Praise for *Obviously Awesome*

"April Dunford is the master at positioning and bringing B2B tech to market. *Obviously Awesome* pulls together two decades of her experience into a brilliant step-by-step book that actually shows us how to do positioning, rather than just talking about it—with great examples and a few chuckles along the way."
Rich Mironov, CEO and product management guru

"In this valuable book, April Dunford proves that products can be transformed by changing their context. *Obviously Awesome* is a must-read for any founder, marketer or salesperson struggling to make their product stand out in crowded markets. We spend a lot of time talking about product and engineering, and not enough time thinking about marketing and positioning—this book can help change that."
Kirk Simpson, co-founder and CEO of Wave

"Three years ago, April Dunford contributed invaluable work for Redgate, helping us position our company around a reframed area with more growth opportunities and a bigger mission than we had before. Since then our revenues have grown substantially, in part due to our better positioning. In her new book, *Obviously Awesome*, April provides an easy-to-understand framework for you to do your own positioning work. If you run through her 10-Step Positioning Process and give yourself the chance to allow the scales to fall from your eyes, you'll improve your positioning and ultimately, your product."
Simon Galbraith, CEO of Redgate Software

"April Dunford is the thought leader across the country and beyond when it comes to marketing and positioning for startups. She has an uncanny ability to see well ahead on how tech companies will be perceived by their users and customers, and has incredible insights for founders as they launch and scale their startups."
Sunil Sharma, managing director of Techstars Toronto and co-host of Collision Conference

"Great positioning is an unbeatable advantage. But you're probably doing it wrong. This book fixes that, offering a clear roadmap that businesses of any size can use to find and communicate their unique advantages on their own terms."

Alistair Croll, founder of Solve for Interesting and bestselling author of *Lean Analytics*

"Positioning. Is. Hard. Really hard. But April Dunford gets it better than anyone I know. Candid, deeply knowledgeable and—just as she is onstage—obviously hilarious. April is a master storyteller, and if you liked her keynote talk, you are going to love this book."

Oli Gardner, co-founder of Unbounce

"April Dunford's two decades of marketing leadership in large companies and small give her a unique perspective on positioning. This how-to guide is a must-read. Before you spend a dollar on sales and marketing, read April's book on positioning."

Renny Monaghan, VP solutions at RingCentral

"Sometimes you need a smart, experienced outsider to help you see things in your business in a different light. April Dunford is that person."

Benjamin Alarie, CEO of Blue J Legal

"April Dunford's product positioning knowledge and experience are voluminous and she has an unparalleled ability to apply them. Before working with her, we really struggled to quickly and simply articulate our value proposition to customers and often left them confused. When we went through her positioning workshop, she was able to help us home in on a place in the landscape and a value to customers that made sense to people immediately. She's distilled the elements of the workshop into this book clearly and simply, making it possible for product marketers and entrepreneurs alike to take themselves through the key steps to successfully positioning your product or company. Highly recommended!"

Jen Evans, CEO and co-founder of SqueezeCMM and president of B2B News Network

"*Obviously Awesome* is the playbook for making your market category work for you instead of against you. If your product is hard for customers to figure out, this book is for you."
Mark Organ, founder and CEO of Influitive, founder and former CEO of Eloqua

"April Dunford may know more about product positioning than any person alive and her deep, practical experience shines in this book. Witty, thoughtful and genuinely useful, *Obviously Awesome* is the must-read bible on positioning. If your product is hard for customers to figure out, this book is for you."
Rich Emrich, CEO of Altus Assessments

"Having an experienced outsider work with you can be really valuable to help you see your business from a new perspective. April Dunford helped us navigate our complex industry landscape and clarify the core of our positioning."
Mazdak Rezvani, founder and CEO of Chatkit

"April Dunford's deep experience working with startups shines in this treasure trove of strategic marketing goodness."
Marie Chevrier Schwartz, founder and CEO of Sampler

"April Dunford has decades of practical and value-driven experience leading teams at early stage companies. There are few go-to-market professionals that have proven scale-up success across multiple organizations. If you are a startup looking for assistance to accelerate your business and learn from someone who has really been there and done that, April's your gal."
David Bloom, founder and CEO of LevelJump

"*Obviously Awesome* is a tremendously valuable guide for marketers at companies of all sizes. April Dunford knows better than just about anyone how much companies struggle to understand the relationship between their product and the context through which their product is viewed by the outside world. This book is perfect for founders, marketers or salespeople who need to move beyond the

basic process of writing down a positioning statement and actually doing the work to make their product stand out in crowded markets."
David McIninch, senior VP strategy and marketing at Fiserv

"You won't meet anyone who understands the art of positioning as deeply as April Dunford. I wish that every founder I worked with would read this. I have no doubt that *Obviously Awesome* will quickly become the de facto reference text on positioning. (Bonus: I literally laughed out loud.)"
Georgiana Laudi, SaaS marketing and growth advisor, startup mentor, former VP marketing at Unbounce

"April Dunford's trademark wit and entertaining style make *Obviously Awesome* easily the best business book of the year. If you want your customer acquisition costs to go down, sales to close faster and your customers to stick around longer, you need to position your products to be 'obviously awesome' too. Move over, Eric Ries and Steve Blank, there's a new must-read book in town for startup founders and executives."
Ashley Greene, CEO and founder of Instratify

"This is marketing mojo in a box. We finally have a book on positioning that is prescriptive and not just descriptive, and April's process really works. Buy the book. Read the book. Use the book."
Rob Tyrie, founder of Ironstone Advisory, formerly global lead for insurance at Salesforce

"April Dunford wisely reminds us that sexy marketing tactics and technologies are, ultimately, at the mercy of the product's positioning. In stepping us through the process to deliver obviously awesome positioning, April gives us a beautiful gift: the ability to align the entire company's efforts behind a winning strategy."
Mitch Solway, fractional CMO for Startups, formerly VP marketing at Vidyard, FreshBooks and Lavalife

OBV!OUSLY
AWESOME

APRIL DUNFORD

OBV!OUSLY AWESOME

How to Nail Product Positioning so Customers Get It, Buy It, Love It

Ambient Press

ISBN 978-1-9990230-0-3 (paperback)
ISBN 978-1-9990230-1-0 (ebook)

Produced by Page two
www.pagetwo.com

Cover design by Peter Cocking
Interior design by Setareh Ashrafologhalai
Interior illustrations by Michelle Clement

19 20 21 22 23   5 4 3 2 1

www.aprildunford.com

You've got a cool product, but nobody understands it. You think it's simple, but customers don't. They compare your products with those that are nothing like it.

At first you think this is a sales or marketing problem. If prospects don't understand what your product is all about, it must be because they haven't really heard you, or you're not saying it clearly enough. But if that were true, then you would see additional marketing result in more sales, and your sales reps wouldn't have to work so hard explaining what your product is and why anyone should care.

CONTENTS

III. PUTTING POSITIONING INTO PLAY

You have
a positioning
problem.
I have a
solution in
10 easy steps.

INTRODUCTION

I frequently speak at tech and marketing conferences, and when I tell organizers I want to talk about positioning, their answer is always the same, "Don't you have something cooler to talk about?"

I get it. Positioning isn't new, and it isn't trendy. You might even think we know everything there is to know about positioning by this point. You'd be wrong. Many of us know what positioning is, but very few understand how to *do* it.

The way we market and sell products is constantly changing. Recently we have seen the emergence of account-based marketing, growth hacking, content marketing, video marketing, visual search, voice search and chatbots. You could forgive any conference organizer for thinking that there are more current and exciting topics out there than positioning. Why do a talk on that old stuff? Why write a book on it? Hey—why even *read* a book on positioning?

Because every single marketing and sales tactic that we use in business today uses positioning as an input and a foundation.

To put it another way—none of the new, cool stuff works without good positioning as a starting point.

Positioning is the act of deliberately defining how you are the best at something that a defined market cares a lot about. Want to do better account-based marketing? Get a better understanding of how to identify your best target accounts.

Want to create better marketing content? Understand your value and differentiators better.

Want to grow revenue faster? Understand what makes a best-fit customer. Positioning is a fundamental input into every tactic we execute, every campaign we launch, every piece of content we create, every sales pitch we make.

If we fail at positioning, we fail at marketing and sales. If we fail at marketing and sales, the entire business fails. Like speaking Japanese slowly and loudly to a person who speaks only English, putting a bigger marketing budget behind confusing and unclear positioning doesn't work. And it's hard to blame the sales process when it takes several meetings for a customer to figure out what your product is, let alone whether or not they want to purchase it.

Weak positioning diminishes the results of everything we do in marketing and sales. It's a wind in our face, constantly slowing us down, making the effort required to meet our business targets just that much more difficult. It's like trying to make an omelet with rotten eggs—your cooking technique is perfect, but nobody wants to eat what you're serving.

"How do you beat Bobby Fischer? You play him at any game but chess."

WARREN BUFFETT

· · · · · · · · · · · · · · · · ·

Great positioning supercharges all of your marketing and sales efforts.

Strong positioning feels like we're cheating. It lets us draft along with the forces of the markets we operate in, making everything we do in marketing and sales easier. No matter what direction we face, the wind is blowing at our back.

But positioning has a positioning problem.

When I talk to people about positioning, we often spend the first part of the conversation reaching a common understanding of positioning. Some folks think of positioning as messaging, and others think everything related to marketing is positioning.

The first step to optimizing positioning is to really understand what it is.

I like to describe positioning as "context setting" for products. When we encounter something new, we will attempt to make sense of it by gathering together all of the little clues we can quickly find to determine how we should think about this new thing. Without that context, products are very difficult to understand, and the whole company suffers—not just the marketing and sales teams.

I've seen startups use a shift in context to transform a product that customers found confusing or irrelevant into an obvious, must-have purchase. I've seen customers struggle to understand products that my team found absurdly simple, and I've seen deeply innovative solutions misunderstood as totally irrelevant. Often, you're too close to your product to realize that the market doesn't think about it the way you do.

Positioning is a secret superpower that, when harnessed correctly, can change the way the world thinks about a problem, a technology or even an entire market.
And yet, there isn't a standard way to position products. Can positioning be taught, or does it need to be done in a different way for every product and audience? Can you be strategic about setting context, or is it all about right place, right time?

The concept of positioning first became a popular marketing construct in 1981 with the publication of *Positioning: The Battle for Your Mind* by Al Ries and Jack Trout. To put that into perspective, in the early 1980s you were likely listening to Blondie's "Call Me" on your new Sony Walkman while you played Pac-Man. That is, if you had even been born.

Ries and Trout argued that markets had become crowded with copycat products, and buyers were overwhelmed with the volume of marketing aimed at them. In order to break through the noise, companies would need to take into account their own strengths and weaknesses, then contrast them with their competitors to create a unique leadership position in the minds of customers.

While Ries and Trout defined what positioning was all about, they didn't give us many clues for how to *do* it. Their case studies focused on TV advertising campaigns their agency had worked on, giving many people the impression that positioning was something best crafted by an agency and executed through big-budget advertising campaigns.

Today, opening the App Store on my smartphone gives me over 2 million choices. One of those apps, Amazon, gives me a marketplace of just under 580 million products to choose from. Not only that, your customers are now exposed to more ads and branding than your Walkman-listening self could have ever imagined. Clear positioning was important in 1981; we are doomed without it today.

Does the world really need another positioning book?

If positioning is so important, and the concept has been around for decades, then surely we know how to do this, right? That's what I thought when I got my first job in marketing and realized I was going to have to figure this out. I learned that there was no shortage of books talking about positioning, but none offered a methodology for actually *doing* it.

That doesn't mean folks were ignoring positioning completely. We were doing it, we just weren't super effective at it.

I repositioned every product I worked on as an executive, all sixteen of them, but I was learning the hard way and making every mistake possible. When I talked with other folks who were doing positioning work, I realized they were doing the same thing: getting it wrong and then trying it differently the next time. In the absence of a process to follow to position a product, we mucked around until we figured it out (and sometimes we didn't figure it out).

After I'd repositioned a dozen or so products, I felt like I was getting pretty good at it and wanted to share my knowledge with others. In my spare time, I served as an entrepreneur in residence (EIR) at a local startup accelerator and started doing positioning sessions one on one with startups. I did a set of guest lectures at three different universities, talking through my ideas on positioning. I spoke at conferences and private events. I built a set of templates and tools. I began teaching a regular masterclass on positioning with a university accelerator, and started offering private sessions to both startups and larger companies across industries. Skeptical tech startup founders and grizzled "been there, done that" marketing and product executives have challenged and refined my technique over the years. My process has been thoroughly field tested and proven as a bulletproof way to connect the customer with the product, leading to sales.

I decided the world did indeed need one more positioning book, one that would share this clear process.

This book will show you how to deliberately position your product to maximize the success of your business. I'm going to show you a simple way to break positioning into components so you can hone and perfect each piece. You will learn how to put those pieces together into a market position that is centered on your strengths and focused on your best-fit customers. You might even start to think that positioning is cool.

So who exactly is this book written for?

- You're the founder, CEO or an executive at a startup that needs prospects to quickly understand why your product is unique and important to shorten your sales cycles and grow revenue.
- You're a marketer who wants to make it easier for your target customers to understand the strengths of your offerings so you can generate more leads.
- You're a salesperson who needs to quickly get prospects to the aha moment where they understand what the product is all about and why they need it.
- You're an executive at a mature business who has seen your growth flatline as your market gets crowded and new competitors nip at your heels.
- You sell products online and you need help connecting with customers who will love your distinctly amazing products.

"Strategy is about making choices, trade-offs; it's about deliberately choosing to be different."

MICHAEL PORTER

• • • • • • • • • • • • •

Above all, you recognize that your business will not succeed if you can't connect product and prospect.

Customers need to be able to easily understand what your product is, why it's special and why it matters to them. When positioning is not working, it often looks like a marketing or sales problem; dig a bit below the surface and you can see that something else is going on.

Weak positioning leaves a trail—the signs are there if you know where to look.

1. **Your current customers love you, but new prospects can't figure out what you're selling.** Do you spend more time explaining what you're selling rather than closing deals? If your prospects can't figure out what you do—quickly—they will invent a position for you, one that potentially hides your key strengths or misrepresents your value. When you don't own your positioning, you are putting your company at a competitive disadvantage. Talk to people—not just friends and family—who would be great prospects for your offering. Show them your product and explain what it does. Now ask them how they would describe what you do. Likewise, ask existing customers about your offering and see what they say. If you see a disconnect between how your happy customers think about your product and how prospects see it, you likely have a positioning problem.

2. **Your company has long sales cycles and low close rates, and you're losing out to the competition.** Do your customers seriously evaluate your product, only to drop out at the last minute? Products with a strong position make their value obvious, attract suitable customers and sell quickly. Effective

positioning makes your sales efforts more efficient by attracting customers who are a great fit and who move through a buying process quickly. Otherwise, poor-fit prospects consume your busy sales team's valuable time, energy and attention—only to choose a competitor that was a better fit for them all along.

3. **You have high customer churn.** Do you have high customer churn shortly after purchase, and new customers who are constantly asking for features you have no plan to deliver? Customers who misunderstood your value chose you for the wrong reasons, and now they're trying to recover sunk costs by turning your product into what they thought they were getting. In a worst-case scenario, your development team may spend time building features for these disappointed customers, trying to appease a group that is likely to quit eventually, while overlooking your happiest customers. Pairing weak positioning with strong marketing and sales efforts leads to customers abandoning your product soon after they have purchased it—particularly bad news for subscription-based businesses that depend on renewals.

4. **You're under price pressure.** Do customers complain that your prices are too high? You can't charge a premium for a product that seems exactly like everything else on the market, and weakly positioned products are seen to offer little beyond their competitors. Clear positioning helps prospects understand that you are a leader in your market segment and that you offer considerable value, making it easier for you to charge a premium.

Positioning is worth it. And it's not that hard.

Obviously Awesome isn't about theory and principles (although I will give you just enough of those to make you dangerous), it's about how to get the job of positioning done, out there in the real world where nobody cares about "best practices" or how things are supposed to work.

You'll learn how to implement a new position for your offerings that will put you at a distinct competitive advantage.

It *is* possible to do positioning effectively and make your product obviously awesome to the customers out there who really need it. So let's figure out what exactly you're trying to sell. But first, let's understand what positioning truly is, and why you're having such a hard time doing it.

1

WHAT IS POSITIONING?

POSITIONING
AS CONTEXT

Context enables people to figure out what's important. Positioning products is a lot like context setting in the opening of a movie.

The opening scene helps the viewer quickly answer a list of basic questions that give context for the story about to unfold. Where are the characters? Who are they, and should the viewer love them or hate them? Is the story going to be sad or scary or funny?

Think of the opening scene in *Apocalypse Now*. You see a dense grove of peaceful palm trees swaying in the breeze. But then you start to notice some smoke coming from the bottom of the screen and a helicopter moves quickly across. The palm trees burst into flames as Jim Morrison says, "This is the end." The setting is no longer a beach in the Caribbean; it's a war in the jungle. The scene slowly shifts from the burning jungle to Martin Sheen's face and you realize you're seeing his traumatic memories. He's smoking, he's drinking, he's got a gun, and your mother would have something to say about the state of that hotel room. He walks over to the window and looks out, and you hear his thoughts. "Saigon. Shit. I'm still only in Saigon. Every time I think I'm gonna wake up back in the jungle." The movie is four minutes and forty-five seconds in, but you have enough context to know what it's all about. It's set in the middle of the Vietnam War, the main character has some serious PTSD, and if you thought this was going to be a two-hour laugh riot, you are dead wrong. Hey, they *did* warn you with the title. The opening scene positions the movie so you can stop wondering about the big questions of where, what, why and who and move onto focusing on the story itself within that context.

When customers encounter a product they have never seen before, they will look for contextual clues to help them figure out what it is, who it's for and why they should care. Taken together, the messaging, pricing, features, branding, partners and customers create context and set the scene for the product.

Context can completely transform the way we think about a product.

A good example of this is the famous context experiment conducted by the *Washington Post*. The experiment involved Joshua Bell, an internationally acclaimed violinist, who at the time was considered the best classical musician in America. *Interview* magazine once said his playing, "does nothing less than tell human beings why they bother to live."

Joshua Bell regularly sells out concert halls where tickets cost $300 or more. For this test of context, he would play the violin outside a busy subway station in Washington, DC, during the morning commute. Would people recognize Bell's extraordinary talent, or would they simply walk past him as they would any other street performer? And more importantly for the experiment, would he make more money than a typical street performer?

Bell performed for forty-five minutes. In that time, 1,070 people passed by, and of those, 27 gave him money, and only 7 paused to listen. His total earnings for the concert: $32.17.

You might argue that the commuters of Washington, DC, may simply be late getting to work and don't carry change. Just because he didn't draw a crowd and he didn't make much money doesn't mean the rushing commuters weren't suddenly inspired to ponder the meaning of their lives.

But the *Washington Post* went further and interviewed people who had experienced the music. It turned out that plenty of them weren't in much of a rush at all—like the man getting a shoe shine in the corner of the plaza or the people lined up to buy lottery tickets at the kiosk twenty feet from Bell. It turns out they weren't any more likely to notice the music. One man buying a lottery ticket that morning later remembered every number he chose but only vaguely recalled the musician as "just a guy trying to make a buck." The owner of the shoe-shine stand complained that the music was too loud and admitted that she had thought about calling the police to make him stop. Clearly these folks had not found a reason to live in Bell's music. Although many people were too rushed to appreciate Bell's playing, nothing else told them that what was happening in the plaza was special enough to stop and take in. Joshua Bell was sabotaged by his context.

Even a world-class product, poorly positioned, can fail.
In the context of a concert hall, Bell is perceived as producing something that is very valuable. He's dressed to perform. He's surrounded by an orchestra on a beautiful stage. The

program tells people what awards he has won. Whereas, when he's playing outside a subway station, everything around him has changed. He's dressed like a street performer and standing beside a garbage can, playing for tips. His product—the music—hasn't changed, but in this context, few people recognize its value.

We rely on context to make sense of a world that is full of street performers and concert hall musicians, and full of millions of products of all shapes and sizes. Context allows us to make thousands of little decisions about what we should pay attention to and what we can simply ignore. Without context to guide us, we would be overwhelmed, maybe even paralyzed by choice.

The situation is even worse when we consider innovative products that people have never encountered before. Think back to the last time you saw something novel—like an iPad or a hoverboard or a drone or a cake pop. How did you make sense of it? Understanding something new is challenging because we don't yet have a frame of reference. When we lack context for a product, the easiest way to create one is by starting with something we already know. When you saw a hoverboard, you may have thought, "Hey, that kid is riding a thing that looks like a skateboard, but he's not pushing with his foot." Or you saw an iPad and thought, "That's like a giant cell phone or a little monitor without a keyboard."

For people who build and sell things, the frame of reference that a potential customer chooses can make or break the business. Coke is much more than just fizzy water in the same way that a concert violinist is more than just a street performer with a fiddle.

"If you're a baker, making bread, you're a baker. If you make the best bread in the world, you're not an artist, but if you bake the bread in the gallery, you're an artist. So the context makes the difference."

MARINA ABRAMOVIĆ

Most products are exceptional only when we understand them within their best frame of reference.

For those of us who make and sell products, the frame of reference that potential customers build around our offerings is critical to staying in business. The trouble is, making sense of all the offerings is becoming an increasingly difficult task. There are too many products, all competing for shrinking attention. With so many other offerings on the market, it's easy for products to get lost in the noise or, worse, completely misunderstood and framed in ways that make them unappealing, redundant or merely unremarkable.

While we understand that context is important, we generally fail to deliberately choose a context because we believe that the context for our product is obvious.

The Two Traps

Product creators often fall into the trap of thinking there is only one way to position an offering, and that we have no ability to shift that contextual frame of reference, especially after we have released it to market. We set out to build something (a new dessert or a new way of doing email, for example) and then almost unconsciously position our offering in that market ("dessert" or "email"). But most products can be positioned in multiple different markets. Your dessert might be better positioned as a snack, and your email solution might make more sense if it were positioned as chat. But because we never thought about positioning our product deliberately, we continue to believe there is only one way to think about it.

Without meaning to, we trap ourselves within our own context. We don't know how to shift the framework to best communicate what our product actually is or what it does. These traps usually take one of two forms.

Trap 1: You are stuck on the idea of what you intended to build, and you don't realize that your product has become something else.

Imagine you're a baker and you decide you're going to make the greatest chocolate cake the world has ever known. You probably weren't aware of it, but the minute you decided your product was "cake," you made a set of critical business decisions before the flour hit the bowl. These include:

1. **Target buyers and where you sell.** You will be selling to folks looking for a fancy dessert, either directly at a bakery or food store, or to restaurants that serve fancy desserts after fancy meals.

2. **Competitive alternatives.** You will be competing with other cakes, ice creams, pies and assorted desserts.

3. **Pricing and margin.** You won't be likely to charge much more than you would for other desserts, since you'll be selling the cake alongside them.

4. **Key product features and roadmap.** Your potential customers eat fancy desserts, so your product differentiators will need to appeal to them (likely high-income restaurant goers, or dinner hosts looking to impress guests). You might make your cake organic or gluten free, or add fancy French salt to your caramel sauce.

Now, suppose that in your process of experimentation, you end up creating a cake that is actually quite small. It's so small you could sell it as a self-contained, single-serving cake, so you put a little wrapper around it. You realize that you've actually made supreme chocolate muffins instead of better chocolate cake.

At first it might not seem like this is much of a change. The product hasn't changed much—it's the same batter—but almost everything else about your business has. Why? Because we changed the mental frame of reference around the product from "cake" to "muffin." That change in context changes everything about the business:

1. **Target buyers and where you sell.** Unlike cakes, muffins are sold at coffee shops and diners.

2. **Competitive alternatives.** You are now competing with donuts, Danishes and bagels.

3. **Pricing and margin.** Muffins sell for a buck or two, and you will be looking to sell a lot of them.

4. **Key product features and roadmap.** You are now fighting for the hearts and minds of a noble class of people who eat chocolate for breakfast. They're likely not worried about gluten or the origin of the salt in your caramel. They might like your muffin larger or with more caramel or maybe they want it deep-fried like a hash brown (you might be laughing, but deep down I think you want to try one of those).

So, if you were the baker, you might not see too much difference between muffins and cake—the product is essentially the same, right? However, choosing to make muffins or cake results in two fundamentally different business models, with different ways of making revenue.

As product creators, we need to understand that the choices we make in positioning and context can have a massive impact on our businesses—for better or worse. Once our product is released into the market, we often fall into the trap of thinking that there is a "default" context around our offering. Our product simply is what we set out to build. However, the road from an idea to a market-ready product is rarely a straight line. After we have an idea of what we want to create—a better email app, a faster database or a yummier chocolate cake—we go through a process of building prototypes, or ugly first versions, that we put in front of prospects to get their feedback. We then incorporate new ideas, adding and removing features based on that feedback. We repeat the cycle, often for months or even years, until we have something that our early customers really seem to love.

Frequently, the product we end up with is not what we started out to build. Our email system seems more like group chat, our database seems more like an analytics platform and our cake has become muffins.

This transformation happens so gradually that we, the product creators, often don't notice it. We still see the product as the thing we set out to build. What else could it possibly be? Customers, though, are often left confused by products that don't seem to match up with the way companies are positioning them. This disconnect leaves customers confused, or worse, they believe that the product is simply poorly conceived and therefore can be ignored and forgotten entirely.

Trap 2: You carefully designed your product for a market, but that market has changed.

Your product exists within a market context—simple enough. Trouble is, markets, and the way customers perceive them, are constantly changing. Markets are made up of competitors who are constantly evolving their offerings, often in response to shifts in technology, customer preferences, economic conditions and regulatory requirements.

Sometimes a product that was well positioned in a market suddenly becomes poorly positioned, not because the product itself has changed, but because markets around the product have shifted.

Suppose again that you're a baker and you've been in the muffin business for a while. Over time, your specialty has become extraordinarily healthy muffins filled with nuts, seeds and dates. You've been positioning your muffin as a great breakfast for folks on a diet who want an alternative to the empty calories of a donut. For years, you've sold your "diet muffin" to pudgy workers from the office next door.

Then a bakery opens across the street and your office workers aren't coming to you as often as they used to. You decide to check out the competition and discover a massive crowd that includes not only your former customers but also buff athletes from the gym down the street and a group of stylish moms. When it's your turn to order, you get what everyone else is ordering. You're stunned to discover the hit product at this bakery is just like yours—it's full of nuts, seeds and dates... the ingredients are almost identical! But this muffin isn't positioned as a "diet muffin." In fact, they don't even call it a muffin. It's a "gluten-free paleo snack."

In this case, you had a great product but failed to adjust the positioning as markets around the product shifted. In the past, healthy eaters might have thought of themselves as "being on a diet," but that concept shifted over time as eating habits changed and trendy diets emerged. Now, your once-popular "diet muffin" seems out of date and irrelevant to bodybuilders and trendy moms and eventually even to schlumpy desk jockeys. You were trapped in your original positioning, even though the market had moved on.

For startups and tech companies, this problem is very common. Our markets are complex, overlapping and shifting rapidly. Our customers operate in a context that is often quite different from our startup or tech bubble. It's easy to miss a shift that impacts nurses, housekeepers, insurance agents, restaurant workers or manufacturers while we're drinking espresso and staring at our MacBooks in our exposed-brick, open-plan offices.

How to Position Your Product like Your Company Depends on It (Hint: It Does)

The common failure in both of these traps is not *deliberately* positioning the product. We stick with a "default" positioning, even when the product changes or the market changes. I believe this happens because we haven't been taught that every product can be positioned in multiple ways and often the best position for a product is not the default. We have never been taught that positioning is a deliberate business choice that requires time, attention and, importantly, a systematic process.

Let's walk through an example that shows the difference between "default" positioning and deliberate positioning.

Take the baker scenario from Trap 1. Suppose you weren't happy with those chocolate muffins, and you're back to the cake idea, only now you're going to revolutionize the whole idea of chocolate cake. You imagine cake that people can eat without a fork. This cake will be portable so people can eat it walking down the street with a coffee in one hand and your portable-cakey-thing in the other.

You work on this idea until you have a prototype that your friends and family love. Your Cake 2.0 is an absolute hit!

You're invited to your local business association to compete in a pitch contest for small business innovators. You hope to win some sweet prize money, not to mention the attention of local coffee shop owners who might want to sell your new cake.

Naturally, you pitch your product the way you think about it in your own head. "I wanted to build an innovative cake product," you explain. "So I invented Cake 2.0. It's like a small piece of cake that you can eat with your hands. I've managed to put a handle on it, well it's a stick, really—so you don't need a fork. What I have is an amazing, innovative cake on a stick!"

But is that really what you built? Is "cake on a stick" the best way to position your cool new thing? Right up front, you set the context for what your product is all about. Your "default" position was cake. But when we think of what makes a better cake, we think of bigger slices, better ingredients and more frosting. The qualities that make your product special aren't qualities that you would normally associate with cake at all. Sticks do not belong in cake. "Cake on a stick" doesn't sound like better cake or innovative cake—it just sounds wrong. It sounds like cake doing things it wasn't meant to do. You've created Frankencake. Who would want to eat that?

If I were the judge in a cake contest, I would choose cake over your new thing, because what you invented is fundamentally not cake.

What you said you built   **What you actually built**

Let's try this again, except this time we're going to deliberately position the product in the best context possible. You need to highlight the aspects of this product that make it really special and in a way that puts those features at the very center of how you position it. Yes, your product contains cake, but it's the stick and the shape that make it amazing. You need to position your product so that the stick and the shape make sense. If you position your product as a lollipop, suddenly the stick and the ball belong. Of course it has a stick. Of course it has a ball. Of course it's a snack and not a dessert. But this isn't just any lollipop, it's a lollipop for grownups, so we made it out of cake. A cake pop is easy to understand and, for coffee-drinking grownups on the go, it's a big improvement over your run-of-the-mill lollipop intended for kids.

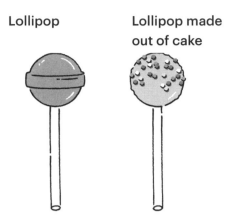

Lollipop

Lollipop made out of cake

We generally fail to consider other—potentially better— ways to position our products because we simply aren't positioning them deliberately.

Cake is a pretty simple example, but we do the same thing with more complex technologies. We decide the context within which our products operate, and in doing so we limit their reach. We don't consider alternative contexts that could make the distinct advantages of our product more obvious to customers.

Positioning Story: From database to data warehouse

Early in my career I worked at a startup founded by a group of folks with PhDs in database technology. Our product was a special kind of database that could quickly find something in a very large collection of data, much faster than the popular databases on the market at the time. We never questioned the way we thought about that product— we were database people and we had built a new kind of database—what else could it be?

The problem, of course, was that at that time the world didn't know it needed a fancy new database. When we met with potential customers and started with "Hi, we'd love to show you our database...," they didn't even let us get to the part where we explained how ours was special and different from the database they already had. They simply didn't want something new, another product to learn, another database to integrate into their existing database systems. Besides, the database they already had was good at a wide range of things beyond analysis, which was our strength. Our sales meetings usually ended early with prospects politely (or sometimes not politely) getting rid of us before we had made it halfway through our pitch.

We spent half our time in every sales meeting trying to explain how our database was different from and better than the database they already had. Sound familiar?
When we tried to find investors for our company, they wouldn't fund us for the same reason: the database market was mature and the big vendors were impossible to beat. There wasn't a need for something new, so how would we grow? Sure, we had one little thing that we were good at, but they didn't believe that was enough for us to win against the existing database companies.

We broke out of this mess by changing our positioning.
It started with a customer telling me he didn't believe we were a database at all. "We aren't?" I said, completely baffled. "What the heck are we?" He went on to explain that in his eyes we were more of a business intelligence tool, or even more specifically, a data warehouse (a specialized

system used for data analysis). This wasn't exactly true in our minds—we lacked some of the features associated with a data warehouse. We did, however, deliver value that was much more clearly aligned with that category of solutions than it was with databases. In fact, in a side-by-side comparison, our database didn't stack up that well against the leading databases on the market, but it blew the doors off the other data warehouses on the market because our analysis capabilities were so superior.

After repositioning our product as a data warehouse, we immediately saw the difference in our first meetings with prospects. Instead of instantly telling us "no, thanks," they now stopped to listen. They stopped comparing us with the database they had already purchased. They intuitively understood the specific problem we could solve and the value to their business. Most importantly, prospects stopped telling us to get lost, and they started buying our solution.

The repositioning didn't stop with marketing and sales—it changed the way we viewed ourselves.
We looked at the features we were planning to build in the future and adjusted them to fit our vision of a warehousing platform. We eventually revised our product roadmap—how should our product reinforce the value we were delivering, and how would we evolve into a better data warehouse? Changing our context not only changed the way customers viewed our product, it changed the way we saw ourselves.

"Find out who you are and do it on purpose."

DOLLY PARTON

Like Joshua Bell delivering a world-class performance in a context that didn't ascribe value, lousy positioning makes your prospects work harder to figure out if you are worth paying attention to. Even if you do manage to capture their attention, ineffective positioning makes it hard for them to understand why they might want to buy what you're selling. How you position your offerings is the underpinning of your entire business strategy and can mean the difference between success and failure.

OK, I'm Sold on Positioning. So How Do I Do It?

Considering how important positioning is, and how long the concept has been around, you would think there's an accepted methodology for doing it. Surprisingly there isn't. At least there isn't one that makes any real sense. (And for those of you wondering where positioning statements fit in all of this, in the next chapter we'll discuss why you should share my intense hatred for positioning statement exercises.)

Great positioning takes into account all of the following:

- The customer's point of view on the problem you solve and the alternative ways of solving that problem.
- The ways you are uniquely different from those alternatives and why that's meaningful for customers.
- The characteristics of a potential customer that really values what you can uniquely deliver.
- The best market context for your product that makes your unique value obvious to those customers who are best suited to your product.

Positioning can be a big and somewhat complex concept. But don't worry, we can make it easier by first breaking it down into its components and then working through each of those in a systematic way.

THE FIVE (PLUS ONE) COMPONENTS OF EFFECTIVE POSITIONING

Positioning is an established concept, yet we have no established way of doing it. We need to start by breaking it down into its components.

We are terrible at positioning because we have never been taught how to do it, or we have been taught positioning through ineffective (and, I think, potentially dangerous) means.

Enter the positioning statement. Somewhere along the way, we have confused teaching people *how to do* positioning with teaching people *how to write down* positioning.

Why You Should Never Create a Positioning Statement

While Ries and Trout did a great job of introducing positioning and explaining why it is important, the closest they came to giving us a map of how to do positioning was to give us a few case studies. The positioning statement filled that gap between theory and practice.

The positioning statement is widely taught in marketing courses and business schools. It's been referenced in many popular business books, including *Crossing the Chasm*, Geoffrey Moore's book on how to market high-tech products, considered *the* business book for entrepreneurs in the 1990s. Even today, companies will come to me having attempted to position their products using the positioning statement and wondering why it's not working.

The first time I encountered the positioning statement as a tool for doing positioning, I was a newly hired marketer at IBM. IBM had a very thorough and detailed release process for new products that included a step called "Positioning." "Great," I thought, "I'm finally going to learn how this positioning stuff is done!" My excitement didn't last long. I soon discovered that the entire positioning process consisted of filling in the blanks of a template that looked something like this:

THE TRADITIONAL POSITIONING STATEMENT		
FOR target buyers, your offering		
IS A market category	**WHICH PROVIDES**	main benefits
UNLIKE primary competitor	**WHICH PROVIDES**	competitor's benefits

I was marketing a database called DB2. DB2 was best known as the leading database platform on a mainframe (that's what we used to call giant, powerful computers back in the olden days). My product was the version of the database that ran on regular computers, and our main differentiator from other databases was that we were IBM—if you were already buying some stuff from us, we could sell you a non-mainframe database while we were at it.

I didn't understand how the positioning statement template was going to help me, so at first I refused to fill it out. My boss politely reminded me that IBM was famous for its product release process and if I enjoyed getting my IBM paycheck, then I should just fill in the darn thing. So I did, and here's what I came up with:

> **THE TRADITIONAL POSITIONING STATEMENT**
>
> **FOR** people who want a non-mainframe database, our non-mainframe database
>
> **IS A** non-mainframe database
>
> **WHICH PROVIDES** an IBM database that runs on platforms other than a mainframe
>
> **UNLIKE** all other non-mainframe databases
>
> **WHICH PROVIDES** everything a non-mainframe database provides.

Useful? Of course not. After I completed the exercise, I filed the statement away and never looked at it again. (Aside: this is where I also first encountered the expression "malicious compliance," meaning you have completed something that was requested of you, simply to illustrate the stupidity of the request.)

The fact that the output of the positioning statement exercise is a hilariously awkward statement of mumbo jumbo isn't even the worst part.

The worst part of a positioning statement exercise is that it assumes you know the answers.

You simply plug in your assumptions as they stand today, and voilà! If you're a baker trying to decide whether to sell cake or muffins, creating a positioning statement doesn't solve your problem. If you're selling a "diet muffin," this exercise doesn't give you any clues that maybe you could reposition your product as a "gluten-free paleo snack." Is my database better positioned as a database or something else? This exercise wouldn't even give me a hint that there are other potential options!

This statement might pass for a way to capture aspects of your positioning, but great positioning is more than just articulating your assumptions around your target market and value proposition. The traditional positioning statement fails in several critical ways:

- **It assumes you know the best way to fill in the blanks.** It might do a good job of capturing your current thinking, but it doesn't give you any clues about whether your positioning is good or bad.

- **It reinforces the status quo.** Most offerings are not explicitly positioned because people believe there is only one possible "default" way to position their product. Rather than helping companies think creatively about what they do, the positioning statement encourages them to look at the market the way they have always looked at it. Status quo thinking will almost always put the existing market leaders at an advantage and leave you blind to potential shifts in the way your customers see your market.

- **It doesn't give you any hints about what to do next.** I've talked to dozens of companies that have gone through the exercise of documenting their positioning statement, and not one did anything useful with it once it was completed. Did marketing refer to it when they created messaging? No. Did the product team use it to inform what features they should build? Nope. Did sales use it to figure out what types of customers they should sell to? Never. What do you call an exercise that produces something that never gets used? A big waste of time, that's what you call it.

- **It's hard to remember.** The structure of the positioning statement makes it difficult to parse or memorize, so even as a way of simply documenting your current thinking, the positioning statement is a complete failure.

As much as I like to complain about the positioning statement as a business tool, there are some things I do like about it. The blanks in the positioning statement cover the aspects of positioning and give us a clue how to break it down into components.

We can break down positioning into five components (plus an optional bonus component) that come together to define what we do, why we are special, which customers we can best serve and the market we intend to win.

These are the Five (Plus One) Components of Effective Positioning:

1. **Competitive alternatives.** What customers would do if your solution didn't exist.

2. **Unique attributes.** The features and capabilities that you have and the alternatives lack.

3. **Value (and proof).** The benefit that those features enable for customers.

4. **Target market characteristics.** The characteristics of a group of buyers that lead them to really care a lot about the value you deliver.

5. **Market category.** The market you describe yourself as being part of, to help customers understand your value.

6. **(Bonus) Relevant trends.** Trends that your target customers understand and/or are interested in that can help make your product more relevant right now.

"You cannot be everything to everyone. If you decide to go north, you cannot go south at the same time."

JEROEN DE FLANDER

• • • • • • • • • • • • • • • • •

1. Competitive alternatives

The positioning statement exercise includes a space for defining a competitor or competing product. For many products, however, there can be several competitive alternatives and not all of them will be "products" per se. Alternatives to your product can be "hire an intern to do it," "use a spreadsheet" or even "suffer along with the problem and do nothing."

The competitive alternative is what your target customers would "use" or "do" if your product didn't exist.
Our customers often do not know nearly as much about the universe of potential solutions to a problem as we do. As product creators, we need to be experts in the different solutions that exist in a market, including the advantages and disadvantages of choosing them. Customers, however, have often never purchased a solution like yours before. They are approaching the solution to their problem with a clean slate and little knowledge of what "state of the art" in your domain looks like. You may worry a lot about an up-and-coming startup in your space, but your customers have likely never heard of them. In business software, the most common competitive alternative is a combination of general-purpose business software (spreadsheets, documents, presentations) and manual processes.

It's important to really understand what customers compare your solution with, because that's the yardstick they use to define "better." For example, your solution might be much easier to use than the product that other startups are selling, but if the real alternative in the mind of a customer is Excel, you can't say your product is easier to use unless it is easier to use than a spreadsheet.

2. Unique attributes

Unique attributes are capabilities or features that your offering has that the competitive alternatives do not have.

Your unique attributes are your secret sauce, the things you can do that the alternatives can't.

It's the list of capabilities that you have and the alternatives don't. For technology companies, these are often technical features, but unique attributes could also be things like your delivery model (such as installed on-premise vs. software as a service), your business model (think Rent the Runway upending retail by leasing instead of selling special-occasion wear) or your specific expertise (perhaps you have a dozen international banks as clients and therefore understand their business better than others in the market). In my database-turned-data-warehouse example, our key unique attribute was our patented query algorithm.

For service businesses—like consultancies, agencies and custom-development shops—the unique attributes are often related to a combination of expertise and experience. For example, you might be the only design and user experience (UX) agency with experience in training design for large enterprises. You could be the only group of Python developers that also has significant experience with retail point-of-sale systems.

Sometimes, traditional positioning statements try to capture this idea under the label "differentiator." In general, you will have many differentiators. The key is to make sure they are different when compared with the capabilities of the real competitive alternatives from a customer's perspective.

3. Value (and proof)

Value is the benefit you can deliver to customers because of your unique attributes. In my earlier example of the database, the value that mapped to our patented algorithm was that companies could get answers from their data in minutes rather than hours, which helped them serve their customers better.

If unique attributes are your secret sauce, then value is the reason why someone might care about your secret sauce. Value should be as fact-based as possible. Qualitative value claims, such as "people enjoy well-designed user interfaces," are too subjective and customers won't believe them. Your opinion of your value does not count as proof; the opinion of customers, reviewers and experts does. Data or third-party opinions are difficult to refute. Your value needs to be provable in an objective and demonstrable way.

4. Target market characteristics

In most cases, the value you provide is at least somewhat relevant to a wide variety of customers. However, if you are a small business you don't have an unlimited marketing budget and a giant army of salespeople. Your sales and marketing efforts have to be focused on the customers who are most likely to buy from you. Your positioning needs to clearly identify who those folks are. And simply put, they are the customers who care the most about the value your product delivers. You need to identify what sets these folks apart. What is it about these customers that makes them love your product more than others? How can we identify them?

net market is the customers who buy quickly, rarely ask for discounts and tell their friends about your offerings. For businesses, big-picture characteristics include things like industry, location and company size, but those are rarely enough to identify a customer who is a great fit for your product. You might sell a solution for small business that greatly reduces the time and complexity of invoicing. Any small business could use your product, but the ones that send a significant number of invoices every month will love you the most.

Suppose your company was running out of cash and if the team didn't close a certain amount of business by the end of the month, very bad things were going to happen. What types of customers would you focus on and why? What are the characteristics of those customers that make them more likely to buy? We originally thought about our database target market as "any company with a very, very large amount of data." But that wasn't specific enough—loads of companies with a large amount of data only store it for backup and don't care about fast analysis. Then we asked ourselves who cares a lot about getting answers *quickly* from a large amount of data. One group was banks that had a very time-sensitive need to analyze data to quickly identify a potential security threat. This specificity of positioning allowed us to be really targeted in our sales and marketing—instead of focusing our marketing on any company with a lot of data, we could specifically target banks.

5. Market category
Think of the market category as a frame of reference for your target customers, which helps them understand your unique

value. Market categories serve as a convenient shorthand that customers use to group similar products together.

Declaring that your product exists in a market category triggers a set of powerful assumptions.

Customers need a way to make sense of the overwhelming number of products on the market. When they are presented with a new product, they will attempt to use what they know to try to figure out what it's all about. Market categories are one way that customers organize products in their minds. Declaring that your product exists in a certain market category will set off a powerful set of assumptions in customers' minds about who your competitors are, what the functionality of the product should be and what the pricing is like.

For example, if I describe my product as "a customer relationship management (CRM) tool," you will assume my competition is Salesforce, because they are the leader in that market. You would assume the features include basic CRM functionality such as keeping track of contacts, activities and opportunities. You would also naturally assume that my pricing is similar to Salesforce, both in the pricing model (a monthly price per user) and the actual cost.

Your market category can work for you or against you.

If you choose your category wisely, all the assumptions are working for you. You don't have to tell customers who your competitors are. It's assumed! You don't have to list every feature, because it's assumed that all products in the category have basic category functions.

However, a poor category choice can turn that power against a product. If the market category we select triggers assumptions that do not apply to our product, then a good portion of our marketing and sales efforts are going to be spent battling those assumptions.

Positioning Story: An email-for-lawyers solution that isn't really email

I once received a call from a startup with a product that customers loved but prospects couldn't figure out. The founders were ex-lawyers who had set out to build "better email for lawyers," and they walked me through a demo. I asked them to show me the calendar and they explained it didn't have one. I was surprised, since calendaring is assumed functionality for any email solution. Interestingly, their happy customers didn't mind. They chose the product for its ability to do secure, context-aware file sharing. Again, I was surprised. File sharing is a problem normally solved with team collaboration software, not email.

The product was positioned as "email" but didn't have features we assume any email solution would have. Also, the key unique feature of the product was not expected or even particularly valued in their market ("email"). Repositioning the product as "team collaboration software" made it easier for customers to intuitively understand what was valuable about it, and avoided customers looking for functionality it didn't have. Even though the product was developed with a certain market in mind, what the company built was a better fit in a completely different market category.

Market categories help customers use what they know to figure out what they don't.
A well-chosen market category will help make your unique value more obvious to your target customers.

6. (Bonus) Relevant trends

Positioning a product within an established market category will help customers quickly understand your product and whether or not they should consider buying it. You should always make it easy for prospects to understand what market category you operate in. But there is another way to give your customers additional context to help them understand why your product is valuable. Used carefully, trends can help customers understand why your offering is something they need to pay attention to right now.

It's easy to confuse market categories and trends, but they are not the same thing. Market categories are a collection of products with similar characteristics. Trends are more like a characteristic itself, but one that happens to be very new and noteworthy at a given point in time.

Market categories help customers understand what your offering is all about and why they should care. Trends help buyers understand why this product is important to them right now. Trends can help business buyers understand how a product aligns with overall company priorities, making it a more strategic and urgent purchase. Trends are important because, as customers, we want to learn about new, interesting and potentially disruptive technologies or approaches. Nobody wants to be left behind when a shift happens, so we're constantly looking out for new developments that might have an impact on us and our business.

"Sit, walk or run, but don't wobble."

ZEN PROVERB

Buyers are always interested in how the world is changing and that makes them interested in trends. Media, blogs, magazines and books cover trends because they are new and interesting to read about. Buyers also worry about disruption and will often be looking to understand new technology and capabilities that they might need to know about or take advantage of for competitive reasons.

Trends can help customers understand why a product is important right now.

Every year, Pantone, inventors of the Pantone Color Matching System, selects a "color of the year." In 2019, it's "living coral" (or pink, for us regular folks). Companies then create pink clothing, lipstick and furniture to be on trend. If you create a pink couch, you are still in the couch business (your market category) but you used a trend (pink) to make it clear that your couch is cool in 2019.

In technology, we can think of market categories as groups of solutions that are similar and compete with each other. Accounting software, group chat, security systems, networking solutions—these are all market categories. Trends in technology can be applied to multiple market categories. Blockchain technology, artificial intelligence (AI) and augmented reality are examples of trends that are relevant to multiple different markets. AI itself is not a market category and tells customers little about what a product is. AI-empowered CRM, however, tells us what the product is (CRM is the market category) and gives us a clue about what makes it special right now (the use of AI).

Using a trend in positioning is optional (but often desirable).
Position your product in a market category that puts your offering's strengths in their best context, and *then* look for relevant trends in your industry that can help customers understand why they should consider this product right now.

Positioning Story: Sampler highlights a trend to help consumer packaged goods companies understand the importance of improved product sampling

Marie Chevrier Schwartz was part of a marketing agency working with large consumer packaged goods companies on product sampling campaigns when she realized that brands were wasting their money. "North American brands spend nearly $10 billion a year handing out product samples in pharmacies, grocery stores, retail stores and street corners," Marie explains, "but they have no way to ensure their samples get to the people most likely to buy, no way to go back to those consumers with offers, and no way to track who loved the product and purchased it later. I knew there had to be a better way." Marie started Sampler, a solution that lets brands target consumers based on age, interests and behaviors; delivers the samples; and tracks redemption rates and customer insights.

The market context for Sampler was obviously "product sampling" but helping customers understand what made Sampler different and better from their current sampling programs proved to be a harder challenge. "When we started we thought of ourselves as 'online product sampling,' which left the brands confused about whether or not we could handle physical product samples. We needed a way to position ourselves that would tie closely to what they already understood, while at the same time make our differentiated value very clear."

There are several big trends impacting consumer brands. New brands like Dollar Shave Club that are skipping traditional retail and building their own relationships with consumers are threatening traditional brands in categories they never thought possible. At the same time, while brands need to sell through Amazon because of its reach with consumers, Amazon also poses a huge threat to them, because it has the power to move into a category armed with its consumer behavior data and quickly dominate it. In response, big consumer brands are investing heavily in building out their own direct-to-consumer strategies that will allow them to build their own relationships with consumers.

"The value of our solution is really well aligned with direct-to-consumer initiatives," Marie explains. "Our solution helps them rapidly build out a targeted buyer list and get deeper insights about consumer behavior and preferences." Sampler adjusted their positioning to describe themselves as "direct-to-consumer sampling" to make the link more explicit.

"When we started to describe ourselves as "direct-to-consumer sampling," brands made Sampler a priority and deals closed faster. Now we can clearly communicate how we tie into one of their most important initiatives—it really makes our solution more strategic to brands." Sampler now works with brands like L'Oréal, Kimberly-Clark and Unilever for samples of everything from moisturizers to granola bars.

Each component has a relationship to the others.

Attributes of your product are only "unique" when compared with competitive alternatives. Those attributes drive the value, which determines who the best target customers are, which in turn highlights which market frame of reference is the best one to highlight your value. Trends must be relevant to your target customers, and can be used in combination with your market category to make your product more relevant to your buyers right now.

Because these relationships flow from one another, the order in which you define the components is very important. I've seen teams start with defining key features, without looking at competitive alternatives, and the resulting positioning doesn't connect with how customers really evaluate a solution. Similarly, I've seen teams start with value or a segmentation and end up with positioning that doesn't click with customers. In the work I've done with startups, I've determined that it's critical to start with understanding what the customer sees as a competitive alternative, and then working through the rest of the components—attributes, value, characteristics, market category, relevant trends—from there. The flow looks something like this:

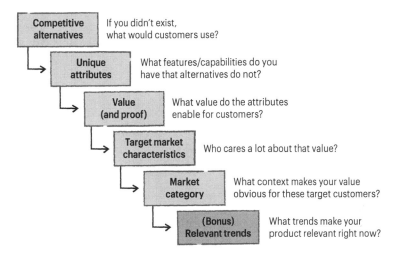

In Part II, I will give you a process for working through the components in the right order.

Defining the Components and Pulling Them Together

Now that you understand each component of positioning, you can work to bring them together to own your market. Ready to learn the 10-Step Positioning Process? Of course you are.

THE 10-STEP POSITIONING PROCESS

STEP I.
Understand the Customers Who Love Your Product

When I started thinking about how to build a systematic approach to positioning, one of the first obstacles I encountered was the interdependencies between the components.

Our best market category depends on who our target customers are and what value we can deliver. The value we deliver depends on our differentiators, which depend on what alternatives we compare our product to. But the market category also tells customers who our competitors are. If everything depends on everything else, where on earth do we start in what seems to be a circular process?

The answer hit me during a coffee meeting with a friend who, like me, had been a VP of marketing at a series of successful startups. He had just joined a new startup and we were chatting about the best course of action to take in the first thirty days at an impatient startup that's looking for fast results from their new executive.

We discovered that our philosophies were strikingly similar—we spent all our time looking for things that work, and then deciphering why. What marketing campaigns brought in the most leads? Which pieces of content were consumed the most? What events had the most attendees? Asking these questions led us to the happiest customers. Once we narrowed in on the happiest customers, we went looking for the reasons they were so satisfied while others were not. What was it about our offering that made them so happy with it, and what was it about those customers that made them such a good fit for us? Answering these questions helped us figure out what our value was, who it was resonating for and why—in other words, it helped us get a start on understanding what our positioning should be.

Your best-fit customers hold the key to understanding what your product is.

Looking back at the first few times I repositioned a product, I kept coming back to our happiest customers and how they thought about us. In one case, we tried to survey all of our customers to see why they loved us, and the results were muddy. There didn't seem to be any patterns in why people picked us. I wondered if the results would look different if I only surveyed the ecstatic fans and left the moderately happy customers out of it. Suddenly a clear pattern emerged: all of our customers could look like these very happy ones if we focused our marketing and sales efforts on companies with characteristics similar to the ecstatic fans.

"There is only
one thing stronger
than all the armies
of the world:
and that is an
idea whose
time has come."

VICTOR HUGO

We increased our growth by concentrating on our best-fit customers.

As I shifted to consulting work, I noticed the same pattern in the tech companies I worked with. Taken as a whole, the customer base often seemed very heterogenous and it was hard to see a pattern in why they chose a product, who they viewed as competitors and what their favorite features were. However, if we sorted out just the best-fit customers, we could clearly see patterns.

The first step in the positioning exercise is to make a short list of your best customers.

They understood your product quickly and bought from you quickly. They became raving fans, referred you to other companies and acted as a reference for you. They represent the perfect type of customer you want to buy from you (at least in the short term). Make a list of them. You will use this list as a reference point for the rest of the exercise.

What if I don't have any super-happy customers yet?

This positioning process assumes you have enough happy customers to see a pattern in who loves your product and why. Until you can see that, you will want to hold off on tightening up your positioning.

Time for a test. In the early days of a company, when you are still learning about what customers love and hate about your offering, you need to get your product in front of a fairly wide set of potential customers. Test your offering on this diverse audience so you can see patterns emerge. Do bigger businesses love your product more than smaller ones? Are businesses in a certain industry more drawn to your product than those in other industries? Are your happiest customers more likely to have certain characteristics? We can guess who loves our product most and why, but frequently our guesses are incorrect. Until we have more experience with real customers, it's better to keep our minds open and our positioning loose, and see what happens.

Think of your product as a fishing net. You have a theory that your net is good for catching grouper, but you haven't fished with it yet so you aren't certain what you might catch. At first, you'll want to go where there are lots of different fish and see what you pull up. If you notice over time you're pulling in a lot of tuna, not grouper, you can move to the tuna spot and do the same amount of work to get a lot more fish. If you had positioned your tuna net as a grouper net in the beginning, you might never have figured out your best positioning. Positioning your net broadly as a "fish net" when you have little market experience is the best way to keep your options open until you have enough customer experience to start seeing patterns.

But I want to start with my product, not my customers!

Your first instinct might be to consider your product and its special features and position around them. Understandable! That's the part you understand—and possibly enjoy—the most. But that's a trap. If we start by laying out our unique features, we are unconsciously comparing ourselves to a set of competitors. The trouble is, we frequently see our competitors much differently than customers see them. I've found this to be particularly true in technology startups that are keeping an eye on other startups in their space that are competing with them for investment dollars. That's fine, and you will have to keep an eye on those threats as your business grows in the future. However, keep in mind that most of your target customers have never heard of you or your rival startups—they simply want to know how your product compares to what they use today. Customer-facing positioning must be centered on a customer frame of reference.

Shouldn't we position our product for customers the same way we position it for investors?

Absolutely not! Investors are investing in what your company will be in the future; customers are buying a solution to a problem they have right now. Investors want to hear your vision for what your company will look like five or ten years from now, and how you intend to be a leader in a large, preferably fast-growing market. Customers, for the most part, are making an immediate decision to spend money they have right now to get immediate value and relieve an immediate pain. They generally aren't that concerned about your plan for getting 1,000 more customers that look just like them (although they do want to know you intend to still be in business in the future). Your plan for the future from a customer's point of view could look confusing, terrifying or both. When investors hear the word "disruption," they see opportunity for new companies to expand and grow. But sometimes customers hear "disruption" as replacing things they have invested in—even though they might be ready to do that in the future, they may not want to think about that today.

In general, your website, your sales and marketing materials, your pricing and even your immediate product roadmap will be designed to serve customers, and therefore should reflect your customer positioning not your investor positioning. Investors will understand that and will also understand that the story in your investor pitch deck may look dramatically different from the story in your sales deck.

The process described in this book has been designed with customers in mind, rather than investors.

Am I positioning my product, my company or both?

Throughout this book I give examples of positioning a product and positioning a company. It's important at the outset that you are clear about what you are trying to position.

Startups generally start with just a single product. If that product is successful, you may add another at some point in the future. It's important to note that many companies become very successful and large with only one main offering. Many of the software brands we love, including Slack, Basecamp, Twilio and Box, are all very large, single-product companies today. Outside of software, brands like Zippo and WD-40 do hundreds of millions in revenue with a single product. Beyond those, most of the big brands we know spent a very long time selling only a single product before they added a second. Crocs sold over a billion dollars of colorful foam shoes before they moved into other types of footwear. Salesforce was a single-product company for over ten years before moving beyond their core CRM offering.

In the early days of a company with a single product, positioning the product and the company as the same thing is the easiest path to establishing a brand in the minds of customers, because there are simply fewer things to remember. It makes sense for single-product companies to have the same name, brand and positioning for the company and the product, simply so customers don't have to figure out two things versus a single thing. If you are a single-product company that currently has a company brand and a product brand, I strongly recommend focusing on your product and putting your energy into marketing and selling that. Customers need to understand product positioning in order to find and evaluate a product. They don't need to know or understand that the company is something separate from that product, when it currently exists to sell only one product.

Companies that have multiple products in the market need to think about product positioning and company positioning as separate but highly linked things. If sold individually, each product will have its own positioning that helps customers understand why they might consider buying it. Company positioning is a broader umbrella that helps customers understand why they should consider multiple offerings from the company.

I get asked a lot if a multi-product company should tackle individual-product positioning or company positioning first. The answer depends partly on how much of your revenue comes from selling a single product versus multiple products and partly on your sales process. If most customers first encounter your company through the purchase of a particular product, I would position that single product first. Sometimes, companies sell a product as a way to start working with a customer and then will sell that same customer additional products to expand their business. In this case, I'd start by positioning the first product because it's the most important to the business. If the company mainly sells a group of products together, I would position the company first, and worry about how much to focus on positioning products individually later.

The positioning process outlined in this book can be used for a single product or for a company. For the most part I will assume you are positioning a product, so if you are tasked with positioning a company you will need to replace "product" with "the entire portfolio of offerings."

Positioning Story: Wave expands beyond "accounting" to "financial services"

Near the end of 2010, Kirk Simpson and James Lochrie launched Wave Accounting, cloud-based accounting software targeted at small business owners who were using spreadsheets, documents and shoeboxes to manage their finances. "We wanted to deliver accounting that was incredibly easy to use and get started with," Kirk explains. "To get these owners off the sidelines, we decided to offer Wave for free, and we could then make money through advertising and offers." Customers loved it, and by 2013, they had over 500,000 businesses using their solution.

As the company grew, however, it became clear that even with hundreds of thousands of businesses, advertising alone wasn't going to get them to their revenue goals. At the same time, Wave started to see shifts in the markets around them. Customers were increasingly adopting digital invoicing with embedded online payments, and were asking for services like payroll and other financial products. "We kept asking ourselves what a small business bank would look like if you could design it from the ground up today," says Kirk. "We started to see ourselves as much more of a financial services provider for small businesses and knew that if we could seamlessly blend financial products into our core accounting software that small businesses would be better served."

That shift in company positioning set off a series of changes across Wave. In 2013 they dropped "Accounting" from their name to simply become "Wave," and their new messaging focused on "managing business finances." Their business model also shifted as they announced new services including payroll and payments that were available on a transaction fee basis, while the core accounting and invoicing remained, as always, free. "When we were 'accounting software,' we sometimes had a hard time getting customers to understand that we provided other products like payroll or payments or now even credit products. As that became more core to our business, it made sense to put that at the center of how we described what we do. Today we're 'financial software.' Most of our new customers still find us when they are looking for accounting or invoicing software, but it's more obvious now that we can also provide them many of the financial products they need to be successful, all deeply embedded into the software." The shift in positioning has helped them grow to over 4 million customers in 2019, tracking more than $200 billion in income and expenses and processing billions of dollars through their platform.

STEP 2.
Form a
Positioning Team

A positioning process works best when it's a team effort, ideally from across different functions within the company. Each team, from sales to marketing to customer success, can bring a unique point of view relative to how customers perceive and experience the product.

Assembling a team often exposes how different groups in your company hold certain assumptions about your attributes, value and target markets. In your first meeting, you need to expose all of those ideas and work through a positioning exercise that aligns the whole team with the desired results. Your goal is to effectively work toward developing a new position for your product that the entire company understands and agrees with.

Who should be there?

The person responsible for the business of that particular product must be in the room and be seen as driving the positioning effort. Positioning is a business strategy exercise—the person who owns the business strategy needs to fully support the positioning, or it's unlikely to be adopted. In startups, the head is the CEO and/or the founders. In larger companies, the head is usually the division or business unit leader and occasionally the head of marketing or head of product.

A positioning exercise that is not a team effort driven by the business leader will fail.
I'm frequently asked if positioning is something that the marketing department should "own." In my experience, the head of marketing is often the first to feel the pain of weak positioning and therefore often kicks off a positioning discussion inside the company. But marketing can't "own" positioning, in the same way marketing can't "own" the overall business strategy. It's simply too broad and too important to live in one silo of the overall company.

Positioning impacts every group in the organization. Consider these outputs that all flow from positioning:

- **Marketing:** messaging, audience targeting and campaign development
- **Sales and business development:** target customer segmentation and account strategy
- **Customer success:** onboarding and account expansion strategy
- **Product and development:** roadmaps and prioritization

Positioning is intertwined with the overall business strategy and therefore needs to be led by the business leader. Because positioning impacts the overall team in significant ways, the leaders of each business function must also agree with and execute the positioning, so they should be involved in developing it. You will also want each group represented because they often hold very different perspectives on competitive

"It's no use
of talking unless
people understand
what you say."

ZORA NEALE HURSTON

alternatives, unique features and the characteristics of a best-fit customer. Marketing, sales and customer success interact with customers at very different points in the buyer journey. Product development may have less direct interaction with customers than other folks in the room, but they will have an important perspective on competitive differentiators and what is and is not possible to do with the product.

You want engagement from every group because you need buy-in from every group.
Although there is great value in having representation from different company functions, you also want to make sure you don't have too many people in the room. In my experience, having one or at most two senior folks from a functional group is enough. With too many people in the room, it's hard to hear from each group and you run the risk of having one or two groups dominate the discussion. I've seen positioning team meetings run well with as few as three people and as many as twelve.

Who will facilitate the discussion?
I have run dozens of positioning workshops and I'm often brought in after internal attempts to tighten positioning have failed. I highly recommend bringing in an experienced facilitator to guide the positioning discussion. Having someone from outside the company facilitate the discussion will make the exercise much more productive and balanced. In the positioning workshops I run, I consistently hear that discussions about bigger strategic issues are difficult without someone from the outside making sure everyone's voice is heard. I also hear how helpful it is for the facilitator to gently challenge long-held assumptions that seem cast in stone and untouchable.

STEP 3.
Align Your Positioning Vocabulary and Let Go of Your Positioning Baggage

In order to consider possible new ways to think about a product, we have to consciously set aside our old ways of thinking about it. To do that, we need a common positioning vocabulary.

For your team to develop a new position, they need a common understanding of the goal and expected outcomes. Some team members might come with preconceived notions about what positioning is and how it should be done. If you have managed to gather the senior team to work on strengthening a product's positioning, the last thing you want is to spend half the day arguing about what the heck positioning is.

In the workshops I run, I set aside the first hour to go over positioning concepts and definitions with the team. At a minimum, the team needs to be on the same page regarding:

- What positioning means and why it is important
- Which components make up a position and how we define each of those
- How market maturity and competitive landscape impact the style of positioning you choose for a product

· · · · · · · · · · · · · · · · · · ·

"We have the power to imagine better."

J.K. ROWLING

Let go of your positioning baggage.

The goal of the 10-Step Positioning Process is to find the *best* position for a product, one that puts the product in the context of a market where it can easily win because the product has obvious benefits over alternatives. If we have always thought of our product in one way—as competing in a particular market, or solving a particular problem—it's hard to see it in any other way.

The reality is that most products can be many things to many types of buyers.

There are lots of examples of products that have historically been sold for one purpose, but as markets shifted, they became better known in a completely different market. Take, for example, Arm & Hammer baking soda. Invented in 1846, baking soda, as the name suggests, was used for baking. The inventors created it in their kitchen and sold it in paper bags. It was wildly popular and the creators slowly grew the business, selling more and more baking soda until Arm & Hammer was truly a household name.

Then, in the 1970s, markets began to shift. As packaged food was on the rise and baking on the decline, sales of baking soda began to flatline. The inventors knew that another feature of baking soda was its ability to absorb odors; indeed, some consumers were already putting open boxes of Arm & Hammer in the fridge to help control bad smells. The company could have decided that odor control was not a market they wanted to be in. After all, would anyone really want to bake with a deodorant? But Arm & Hammer decided to let go of the past and focus on markets where they could be successful in the future. They started advertising their current product as a deodorizer for refrigerators and later launched packaging specifically designed for use in a fridge. Converted consumers were now buying a new box every thirty days.

The repositioning drove product sales from $16 million in 1969 to over $318 million by 1987. The repositioning led to other innovations as well—as Arm & Hammer became known as a deodorizer, the brand naturally extended to products for deodorizing everything from cat litter to underarms.

The starting point of this growth was Arm & Hammer's willingness to let go of their old way of thinking about the product.

Freeing your mind from patterns of the past isn't always easy. Thoughts about the evolution of a product, from its conception to launch, are often baked into the initial positioning. Customers don't have the same baggage—they know nothing about the history of the product when they first encounter it.

Market confusion starts with our disconnect between understanding the product as product creators, and understanding the product as customers first perceive it.

The positioning team needs to understand the concept of "positioning baggage" before they can attempt to let go of it. You might find that each team member has a different level of positioning baggage—founders and long-time employees might view the product from the full perspective of its history, while newer employees do not.

Start by calling out where your history appears in your current positioning. Is your current market the one identified when you imagined the product? Do you use terminology and describe features in the same way as when you started? Being conscious of the presence of your history in your current position will help everyone be open to alternatives.

The most important part of this step is to get agreement from the team that, although the product was created with a certain market and audience in mind, it may no longer be best positioned that way. The team needs to agree to suspend their opinions about the positioning of the product for the duration of the exercise so they can be open to new ideas.

Positioning Story: Clearpath Robotics steering robots toward autonomous vehicles

Clearpath Robotics was founded by a group of friends with a shared love of robots. The business began providing solutions that made it easier to do robotics research, a pain they felt themselves in university when messing around with robots in the lab. They eventually came up with a new idea: a robot that could be used in industrial facilities to move around intelligently, picking up and delivering materials.

Having stretched the idea of what a robot could do in a manufacturing environment, Clearpath's next challenge was to create context help their customers understand the robot. "Our systems go way beyond those of a traditional manufacturing robot," says director of product, Simon Drexler. "Traditional robotics are stationary and complete repetitive tasks. Our products move around using mapping and mobile sensor technology. Concepts like 'dispatch' and 'fleet management' are not associated with stationary manufacturing robots."

In other words, every time Clearpath started a conversation with a manufacturing prospect, they positioned their product as "a robot," but then proceeded to explain why their robots were nothing like the robots that manufacturers were used to. Positioning themselves in the robot category put them in direct comparison with other robot vendors whose solutions were nothing like Clearpath's offering. Confused customers were then left to try to figure out how a roving, intelligent, movement-and-delivery solution fit into their current set of assumptions about robots' capabilities. Clearpath needed to create a new way of thinking to help customers understand what was so special about their offering.

Clearpath's innovation was their ability to autonomously navigate around a space in an intelligent and dynamic manner. To many people, that sounds like what a self-driving car does. Clearpath decided there was a new way to think about what they do. They were creating self-driving vehicles for industrial uses. To drive home this positioning, they created a new division called OTTO Motors and enhanced their industrial design to add white "headlights" and red "taillights" to their vehicles. Their website and sales materials look more like what you would see from a car manufacturer than a robotics tech startup.

This shift in thinking had a big impact on their business. It made their unique strengths—mobility, mapping, dispatch, fleet management—central to their positioning and completely obvious to customers. Not only did their sales accelerate, but investors took notice and after their repositioning, they raised $30 million to accelerate their growth. They even won Silver at the prestigious Edison Awards honoring innovations and innovators.

STEP 4.
List Your True Competitive Alternatives

Customers don't always see competitors the same way we do, and their opinion is the only one that matters for positioning.

It's natural for product creators to start by looking at the product and its features to determine the best market, and then build a context around that. As product people, it's often the place where we feel most comfortable. After all, who knows more about our solution than us? But you need to look at those features from a customer's point of view.

The features of our product and the value they provide are only unique, interesting and valuable when a customer perceives them in relation to alternatives.
Although every component of positioning is related to other components, the foundation is the problem your customers are trying to solve, and how they perceive your offering in comparison with other ways of solving the problem.

If problems are the root, why not start by asking customers what problems they're trying to solve? Customers, although well-versed in their problems, are often terrible at describing them in a way that gives product creators enough nuance to make decisions. For example, at one startup I worked at, we asked customers what problem they were trying to solve by using our database product. Our users were generally database administrators, and their answers were typically quite specific and technical: "We just want to run a fast query" or "We have to produce a report, so we need to retrieve data from a very large database very quickly." From those answers, I could assume they viewed our database as one that can quickly execute queries. But when we asked them what they would use if our database didn't exist, none of them named another database; instead, they suggested business intelligence tools or data warehouses.

Understanding the customer's problem wasn't enough—to really understand how they perceived our strengths and weaknesses, we needed to understand the alternatives to which they compared us. Customers always group solutions in categories, but talking to them about problems doesn't necessarily reveal those categories.

You need to create a position that highlights the unique strengths of your product as customers perceive them. To do that, you need to understand who your real competitors are in the minds of customers. Many companies have weak positioning precisely because they don't clearly understand their true competitive alternatives in the minds of customers.

Understand what a customer might replace you with in order to understand how they categorize your solution.

The best way to understand competitive alternatives is to answer the question, What would our best customers do if we didn't exist? The answer could be that they would use another product that looks like a direct competitor with you. But often that's not the case. For many new products, the answer is "use a pen and paper" or "hire an intern to do it." Some of the start-ups I work with have ideas so innovative that customers don't even understand that they have a problem—if the product didn't exist, they would simply "do nothing."

When I go through this exercise in workshops, teams will often want to create an exhaustive list of every possible alternative. That's fine, but I encourage the team to (1) remain focused on the best-fit customer list and name only what those customers would see as an alternative, and (2) rank the list from most common to least common. This way, the team focuses on the most common alternatives and won't worry as much about rare ones.

Focus on your best customers and what they would identify as alternative solutions.
You may have some edge-case customers who are aware of smaller companies or who have a unique reason for considering an alternative, but you're trying to focus on the general case for your best customers.

Don't forget that you are an expert in solutions in this space and quite likely understand the real competitive landscape much better than customers do. If a competitor has a small number of customers, they are likely to have zero mindshare with prospects and should not be listed as a real competitive alternative. Would a customer really use them if you didn't exist? Probably not, since few of them are doing so today. What would the majority of your best customers really do?

The competitive alternatives often naturally cluster, and if so, it's helpful to group them. For example, there might be a group called "do it manually" that includes "hire an intern" and "do it myself with Excel" and another group called "use a small-business accounting solution" that includes QuickBooks, FreshBooks, etcetera. Grouping the alternatives helps the team move to the next step. In my experience, teams usually end up with a minimum of two and a maximum of five groups of alternatives.

STEP 5.
Isolate Your Unique Attributes or Features

Strong positioning is centered on what a product does best. Once you have a list of competitive alternatives, the next step is to isolate what makes you different and better than those alternatives.

In this step you need to stay focused on features and capabilities (also called attributes), rather than the value that those features drive for customers (we will get to that in Step 6). I define features as something your product or company has or does. Some examples of features: "a 15-megapixel camera," "integrates with QuickBooks," "one-click installation" and "metal construction."

In this step, list all of the capabilities you have that the alternatives do not.
List every attribute you can think of, even if it seems like it could be a negative to certain customers and even if you're uncertain what its value might be. For tech companies, patented

features are an obvious place to start. Sometimes it is helpful to think about the feedback you get from customers when you ask them why they chose your offering. You might be the only consulting business with a certain combination of skills and experience. You might be the only company with a certain technology or a certain set of partnerships. You might be the only hat maker that sources materials from Canada or the only makeup that is made from herbs grown in your own organic garden.

It's OK to list things here that some folks on the team might think of as negative. A software company in one of my workshops talked about how they were the only company on the market that required a professional services team to come onsite to install the software. The head of sales felt that was a negative, because it took longer for a company to get up and running with the software. The head of customer service saw it as a uniquely positive attribute, because certain customers wanted that type of customization and high-touch service.

Your opinion of your own strengths is irrelevant without proof.

Some groups at this stage will list features that are either difficult to prove or really more of a benefit than a feature. "We provide outstanding customer service" is probably the most common of these, followed by "very easy to use." Focus on the characteristics of your product or company that drives a potential benefit—ideally those features are based on objective facts and are provable. For example, I have yet to meet a company that believes they provide terrible customer service. If you truly believe that your company is better at customer service, how would you go about proving that? Do you have

"We don't know who discovered water, but we're certain it wasn't a fish."

JOHN CULKIN

more support people than your competitors and can you prove it? Do your support people have certifications that others don't? Ease of use is another "feature" that I believe is really a value. What is it about your product that makes it easier to use and how do you prove it? Do your competitors' products require training and your product doesn't? Can you quantify how long it takes to become proficient with your product versus alternative products?

Third-party validation that your product's feature is better than the alternative counts as proof. If an independent reviewer or analyst stated that your product is easier to use, that's a fact. If a customer says in an approved quote that your customer service is much better than another company's, that's proof.

Be broad and creative with the attributes you list. They could be a proprietary process, expertise in a special area, distribution channels, partnerships or special skills. Tech companies usually think of features first, but it is helpful to dig deeper into the full range of what makes the offering and the company unique. For service companies, the skills of the team are the obvious choice, but experience with a particular kind of project or company can also be a powerful attribute.

Concentrate on "consideration" rather than "retention" attributes.

Consideration attributes are things that customers care about when they are evaluating whether or not to make a purchase. Every product has features that you can connect directly to a goal the customer would like to accomplish right now. Retention attributes are features that aren't as important when a customer is making an initial purchase decision, but are very important when it comes time to renew. These include how easy it is to do business with a company and the quality of customer support.

I'm not saying that positioning doesn't matter for retention—it absolutely does. Poorly positioned products are often bought by customers who misunderstand the real value of a product; those customers often quickly abandon the product when they realize it doesn't do what they thought it did. However, customers who don't see enough value to consider buying the product will never stick around long enough to experience retention attributes such as your excellent customer service.

List as many attributes as you like at this stage. You'll group them as you move to the next stage in the process. Focus on capturing the broader set without trying to decide what's really important and what isn't.

STEP 6.
Map the Attributes to Value "Themes"

Attributes or features are a starting point, but what customers care about is what those features can do for them.

Attributes like "15-megapixel camera" or "all-metal construction" enable benefits for customers such as "sharper images" or "a stronger frame." Articulating value takes the benefits one step further: putting benefits into the context of a goal the customer is trying to achieve.

Value could be "photos that are sharp even when printed or zoomed in," "a frame that saves you money on replacements," "every level of the organization knows the status of key metrics" or "help is immediately available across every time zone."

Features enable benefits, which can be translated into value in unique customer terms.

In this step, you'll capture the value that each of your unique attributes enables for customers. Each feature can have multiple value points, and a combination of features can provide value as well. In Step 7, we'll determine which customers find these valuable and how many of those customers there might be.

Table 1. Features mapped to benefit and value

Feature: Something your product does or has	Benefit: What the feature enables for customers	Value: How this feature maps to a goal the customer is trying to achieve
15-megapixel camera	Sharp photo images	Images can be zoomed in or printed in large format and still look sharp.
All-metal construction	A stronger frame that resists damage	The frame lasts five times longer, allowing savings of $50,000 per year on frame replacements.
One-click reports	Fast, easy report generation	Every part of the organization can make better decisions based on accurate, up-to-date metrics.
24-hour support	Support that is always available	Global operations have access to help across every time zone.

Moving from "features" to "benefits" and then to "value" often confuses people, particularly folks who come from a technical background. An engineer by training, I often viewed features and the benefits derived from those features as interchangeable early in my career. For many consumer technical products, features are presented as valuable in their own right—but only because we do the translation to value automatically in our heads. For example, phone makers have often represented the quality of their cameras by talking about the number of megapixels. Consumers have been trained to translate megapixels to photo quality and therefore believe that cameras with more megapixels take better photos. Digging a bit deeper, the value of "better photos" for most consumers means sharper, more detailed images when printed or zoomed in.

For most of our products, however, we don't have the luxury of letting customers figure out the value of our features on their own. If I tell someone I have a "patented fuzzy logic algorithm" for my product, I would expect their response to be, So what? I explained the feature without being explicit about why it matters. In this example, the benefit might be "faster response times." Taking the question further, What does that mean for customers? What can they do with a faster response time that they couldn't with a slower response? The answer might be that they can use the system to respond to their own customers while a customer is on the phone, rather than having to call them back, thereby decreasing support response times and increasing their customers' satisfaction.

Clustering the Value into "Themes"

In your list, you should see a handful of themes start to emerge and the value those features deliver to customers. Now we need to organize the list.

To group points of value, you need to take the perspective of a customer. What points would naturally be related in the minds of your customers and prospects? For example, if you have attributes like "works on any mobile device" or "works without an internet connection," those might both provide value to customers who would like to use the solution with field workers in remote locations or locations with intermittent Wi-Fi or cell access. You could clump those attributes in a group called "supports remote environments."

Group attributes that provide similar value so you can get down to a more reasonable number. The goal of this step is to see the patterns and shorten the list to one to four value clusters. It's not uncommon for this exercise to produce just a single value point.

"The stone age didn't end because they ran out of stones."

UNKNOWN

. . . .

Remember: this positioning exercise is not about highlighting every little feature and attribute that our customers love. In positioning a product, we're taking the most critical things that make us special and worth considering, and bringing the resulting unique value to the front and center.

STEP 7.
Determine Who Cares a Lot

Once you have a good understanding of the value that your product delivers versus other alternatives, you can look at which customers really care a lot about that value.

It's important to remember that although you have unique attributes that deliver value to customers, not all customers care about that value in exactly the same way. You might have a solution for invoicing that supports integration with an accounting package like QuickBooks. This feature provides the value of saving time and reducing errors from manually entering data. For customers who don't use QuickBooks, the value is irrelevant. Among those who do, customers who send a large number of invoices will feel the pain of data entry more than customers who send only one or two invoices a day. The customers who send a lot of invoices will care a lot about the value of reducing time and errors.

Marketers call this step a "segmentation" exercise. In my experience, if there's a marketing concept more widely misunderstood than positioning, it's segmentation.

Most marketing courses talk about segmentation in a way that only makes sense to large companies who sell to consumers. Segmentation examples are usually based on consumer demographics—for example, "this product is aimed at single men between the ages of 18 and 30." Demographic thinking often bleeds into the way people typically think of segmenting a market of businesses—for example, "small businesses" or "businesses with 100 to 2,000 employees." A useful segmentation, however, needs to go well beyond demographics or firmographics.

An actionable segmentation captures a list of a person's or company's easily identifiable characteristics that make them really care about what you do.
For consumers, a segmentation could include combinations of things such as other brands they own or like, stores they buy from, the job they hold or their music or entertainment preferences. For businesses, it could be the way they sell, other products they have invested in or the skills they have or don't have inside their company.

In this step, you'll determine what makes some prospects much more excited about your offerings than others—think of these as your "best-fit prospects."

Best-fit customers are easiest to sell to and retain.
Focusing on a best-fit prospect segment doesn't always make sense to people who don't have a marketing background. If I wanted to increase my chances of landing a customer, wouldn't I want to target as broad a market as possible? The reality is the exact opposite. The broader your focus, the more difficult it is to connect with prospects and convince them that your solution is the best one for them above all others.

Think about the difference between your best-fit customers and your other customers. Your other customers think your product is OK for the price, but they will jump ship if a different company offers a cheaper or better version. These customers are harder to close business with—they take their time making a purchase decision and frequently ask for a discount. In short, they like your product but they just don't love it. You can target your marketing and sales programs at them, but selling to them and keeping them happy isn't going to be easy.

Now think about your best customers. Everything about doing business with them is different. They understood your product immediately and couldn't wait to get their hands on it. They bought quickly and instead of asking for a cheaper price, they might have told you your product should be priced higher. They tell their friends about your product, and not only do they not churn, they will fight anyone who tries to take it away from them. They don't just like your product, they *loooooove* it. Marketing and selling to these folks doesn't take much effort once you've found them—they are "buying" as much as you are "selling."

If you have limited marketing and sales resources (and let's face it, almost all of us do, even if our business is large), it makes sense to spend them on prospects that are most like your best-fit customers, provided there are enough of them to meet your sales objectives.

Target as narrowly as you can to meet your near-term sales objectives. You can broaden the targets later.
I encourage teams not to get their positioning too far ahead of their business objectives. Think about your sales targets for this year and how many sales you need to make to achieve them. Could you hit your targets by focusing on only your

best-fit customers? If the answer is no, you need to broaden your definition of "best-fit." If the answer is yes, keeping your positioning focused on that segment is the most efficient use of your sales resources and the fastest and easiest path to hitting your sales targets.

Keep in mind that your product positioning will constantly be evolving. There is no need to make sure that your positioning will fit perfectly with where you or your product will be in ten years or five years or even two years from now. Similarly, your target customers will also evolve over time. Great positioning resonates with your best-fit customers right now, and will evolve with them over time.

Many companies take a logical approach to this step, based on what they already know about who values what. For example, companies in highly regulated markets have to care more about information security; managers with very large teams struggle more with team communication and collaboration; smaller companies without in-house IT support need solutions that are easy to set up and run, etcetera.

I've found that this step tends to be either the easiest or the most difficult to work through. You are mapping the value that your product's features deliver to a group of customers who have the highest affinity for your product. You need to focus on the value points that you listed in the previous step and repeat the question, Who cares and why?

For example, your unique feature might be that your online appointment scheduling software supports scheduling across multiple locations and multiple service organizations. The value is that customers can book an appointment at a location that is convenient for them and with a representative that can serve them best. What kind of business cares a lot about that? You might say businesses with a lot of locations and many kinds of offerings. But not all businesses care about appointments. Drugstores have a lot of locations and many offerings, but they don't care that much about appointments. What sort of businesses do? You might list businesses that offer financial services and tax preparation services.

A segment can be defined by narrowing the set of buyers you are targeting. For example, you might focus the category of "accounting software" to "accounting software for freelancers or lawyers." You might narrow down "sporting goods" to "sporting goods for babies" or "for dogs" or "for octogenarians." In general, the segment needs to meet at least two criteria to be worthy of focus: (1) it needs to be big enough that it's possible to meet the goals of your business, and (2) it needs to have important, specific, unmet needs that are common to the segment. If you're a tennis racquet maker and decide to market a racquet for seniors, you need to figure out first if there are enough tennis-playing seniors who might need a racquet, and second if you could fulfil an unmet need that seniors have in their racquets.

STEP 8.
Find a Market Frame of Reference That Puts Your Strengths at the Center and Determine *How* to Position in It

You now have a good handle on your ideal prospects, your product's unique attributes and the value those attributes can deliver. The next step is to pick a market frame of reference that makes your value obvious to the segments who care the most about that value.

Picking a market that does this is harder than you might think. Chances are, when you first conceived the offering, you had a market in mind. You were building an email system for lawyers, a bicycle that could give you directions, a robot that could move things around a manufacturing plant. Baked in was the idea of the market—"database," "bicycle" and "robot" are all markets that exist and mean something to customers. However, since your offering evolved and the market itself evolved over time, the original market category may no longer be the best way to frame your unique strengths. Also, the customers most likely to buy your product might have a very different point of view on markets than you do.

In the context of this exercise, a "market" needs to be something that already exists in the minds of customers (except in the very rare case where you make a conscious decision to create a new market—which we'll discuss later in this step). We position our offering in a market to trigger a set of assumptions—about competitors, features and pricing—that work to our advantage. By choosing to position within a specific market, you're giving your prospects clues about what products they should compare you with, your key features, your price and your benefits. Those comparisons help customers quickly figure out what your product is all about and whether or not they should consider purchasing it.

In Step 3, you let go of your "default" market—part of your positioning baggage—which was most likely the place where you started. Now you are looking to deliberately choose a market frame of reference that makes your value obvious to the folks who care about it the most. There are a few ways to go about this:

- **Use abductive reasoning.** The adage "if it looks like a duck, swims like a duck and quacks like a duck, then it probably is a duck" also applies to new products. With abductive reasoning, you choose a market category by isolating your key features and their value, and asking yourself, What types of products typically have those features? What category of products typically deliver that value?

- **Examine adjacent (growing) markets.** Another place to look for options is in the markets adjacent to the one in which you have been positioning yourself. Frequently, there are overlaps or blurry lines between markets. As a product shifts over time, its features and value could look more at home in a neighboring market. Especially in the tech space, it's not unusual for lines between markets to shift or be redrawn as companies emerge, release new technology or come up with new ideas. Looking at adjacent markets is a good way to find markets that might make your value more obvious to prospects.

Pay particular attention to adjacent markets that are growing quickly. Positioning yourself in a growing market has obvious benefits: a rising tide of customer interest, media focus and buzz, and the appearance of being new and cool—who doesn't want that? But be careful—simply wanting to belong in a market doesn't make it the right one for you. Only choose a market if it makes your strengths obvious.

- **Ask your customers (but be cautious).** I've had folks ask me, "Can't you just ask your customers what market you're in?" My answer: "Sometimes." If you have already positioned yourself in a given market, your customers will have at least attempted to place you there, even if that attempt confused them. They will naturally try to put you in markets that are close to that market. That was the case with our database—a customer described us as an analytics tool because he had been looking at analytics tools and was familiar with them. This market was closely associated with the database market and therefore it wasn't much of a leap for him to think of us that way.

  I would caution you to be extremely careful in seeking feedback from customers and prospects about what market they see you in. Prospects may see things differently than those who have already tried to make sense of your product one way and failed. Also, customers will *only* try to position you in markets that are frequently linked to their industry or job function. Customers aren't positioning experts, nor are they experts in how a market category works. Frequently they will attempt to position you in the most obvious market possible, and this market is often not the best one for highlighting your strengths.

Positioning Story: Wattpad transforms a story platform into an entertainment company

In 2006 Allen Lau and Ivan Yuen shared a vision that as mobile phones became more popular, people would want to read on them. This might seem obvious today, but phones of that era had tiny screens and most people didn't even have data plans. However, that year Motorola launched the Razr with a screen that was much bigger than the popular Nokia phones at the time, and Allen and Ivan predicted that screens would soon be big enough to accommodate reading comfortably. They launched their social storytelling platform, Wattpad, in 2006 to give writers a way to create stories on the web and share them with other people on their phones.

The company grew slowly at first, until the launch of Apple's iPhone forever changed how people use mobile screens. The iPhone's larger screen made reading and writing on a phone not just possible but convenient and comfortable. With the launch of Apple's App Store in 2009, Wattpad began to take off. "When we started we were in the early days of social media," explains Allen, "but by 2010 people were increasingly sharing on the internet and we went through a period of extremely rapid user growth."

Like with many social platforms, Wattpad's founders deliberately decided not to focus on monetization and instead focused all of their efforts on growing a vibrant community of writers and readers. Although advertising brought in revenue, Allen knew Wattpad could be something more. "Even as early as 2012 we knew that our platform was creating a huge number of incredible, well-loved stories. We knew we could do more with them off the platform, potentially adapting stories for TV and movies. It dawned on me that we were much more than a platform for writing and reading, and if we reached the right scale we could become an entertainment company," says Allen.

In 2014 Wattpad got an opportunity to test what was possible when Allen and Ivan were approached by one of the largest TV stations in the Philippines about collaborating on a TV series. "Wattpad is incredibly popular in the Philippines and the TV station wanted to produce a TV drama based on popular Wattpad stories. We saw this as an opportunity to test what we could do. Could we use our data and insight into what readers love to create a better story for TV? Could we help build the TV audience for a show by having a connection with Wattpad readers who were already fans?" The experiment proved to be a major success and *Wattpad Presents* went on to increase the station's viewership by a whopping 30%. The series was a smash hit in the Philippines, running for four seasons and 250 episodes.

In 2016 Wattpad unveiled Wattpad Studios and their new positioning as a global multi-platform entertainment company. "We are now working with media brands like NBC, Sony, Hulu, iflix, eOne and many others," says Allen. "We have 70 million monthly users. Our data can not only help media companies build an audience and promote content, our insight into what audiences love helps find new IP that resonates with fans. We can bring a data-backed approach to developing TV shows and film, using machine learning to guide how decisions get made in the adaptation process. We are completely changing the way the entertainment industry sources and produces content."

There are different approaches for isolating, targeting and winning a market—and certain styles work better for some than others.

Picking a market is like giving customers an answer to the question, What are you? Frequently, however, we need to think a little bit deeper about how we intend to win in the market we have chosen. At a high level we can either choose to enter an existing market or create a new market. If we choose to enter an existing market, we can either compete to win the entire market or position our product to win a slice of it. The "style" of positioning you choose will depend on a set of factors including the competitive landscape and your business goals. Here's my advice on how and when to use each of them:

1. **Head to Head: Positioning to win an existing market**

   You are aiming to be the leader in a market category that already exists in the minds of customers. If there is an established leader, your goal is to beat them at their own game by convincing customers that you are the best at delivering the solution.

2. **Big Fish, Small Pond: Positioning to win a subsegment of an existing market**

   You are aiming to dominate a piece of an existing market category. Your goal is not to take on the overall market leaders directly, but to win in a well-defined segment of the market. You do this by targeting buyers in a subsegment of the broader market who have different requirements that are not being met by the current overall market leader.

3. **Create a New Game: Positioning to win a market you create**

   You are aiming to create a new market category. Your goals are first to prove to customers that a new market category deserves to exist, then to define the parameters of that market in the minds of customers, and lastly, to position yourself as the leader within it.

1. Head to Head: Positioning to win an existing market

You are competing directly against other established players in a well-defined market. For the most part, customers are well educated about what solutions in this market can and cannot do. Prospects also understand the purchase criteria (what is important to consider when making a purchase and what is not).

"If you don't like being a doormat, then get off the floor."

ANONYMOUS

You aren't claiming to be better for a certain type of customer; you're claiming to be better for most, if not all, customers. You're accepting the current way the market category is defined, as well as the current set of evaluation criteria. You aren't trying to change the game; you are winning—or attempting to win—at the game the way it is currently played.

You don't have to explain to prospects what the market is all about; they already know what it is. For example, we know what cola is and we have a set of assumptions about what it's like: brown, fizzy and sweet. Things that aren't brown, fizzy and sweet just aren't cola at all.

Well-defined markets also have generally accepted purchase criteria. If I'm buying a chocolate cake, I know what makes a good one: fresh, chocolatey, generous frosting. When I'm buying a new laptop, I'm looking at screen size, weight, amount of memory and processor speed, and I'm weighing those features against how much I'm willing to pay.

When to use the Head to Head style

If you are already the leader in the market, the status quo suits you. The way prospects define the market has worked well for you (you are the leader here after all!), and you would like them to continue to define it that way. Similarly, the way they currently make decisions about what to buy seems to your advantage. Prospects are comparing alternatives using a set of features where you come out on top.

If you are launching a new product, particularly if you are a small business just starting out, the Head to Head style is rarely a good choice. Trying to beat an established market leader at their own game is a bit like trying to out-cola Coke. It would be foolish for a small company to ever try.

A larger company might attempt to take on an established leader head to head, but only where the market sands are shifting in a way that could put the leader at a disadvantage or a challenger at an advantage. A new breakthrough capability, a change in government regulations or a shift in economic factors might give a strong challenger the opportunity they need to take down an established leader. Without a clear competitive advantage, however, even a large company will have to be prepared to fight hard for every win and cross their fingers for the leader to make a mistake.

The only case where a company might want to position a new product in a known category is when the category itself is defined and understood by buyers, but a strong leader has not yet been established. In technology we see this in new and emerging market categories. For example, "smart glasses" for consumers have been on the market for years and many people understand the basic functionality of smart glasses as being a sort of wearable display and/or camera. Some folks can name a handful of vendors that sell them (Epson or North might come to mind), but most people would be hard-pressed to name a "leader" in this market. In this case, North doesn't need to create an entirely new category from scratch (although it certainly has the opportunity to shape the details of what customers expect from products within it), and it can position itself to be the leader of the entire market, since no clear leader exists yet.

The advantage of positioning in an existing market category is that you don't have to convince people the category needs to exist.
You also benefit from the assumptions that the category brings to mind for prospects. The bonus is you get all of that without having to fight directly with an established leader.

To use this style of positioning, first you have to determine whether or not the category has indeed been created in the minds of customers. You need data that tells you unequivocally that the market already exists in the minds of a critical mass of buyers or is emerging quickly enough for you to meet your business goals. For technology companies in particular, we often assume our knowledge of technology and trends isn't that far ahead of average buyers, when it can be years ahead. That's OK, as long as you're comfortable knowing that enough buyers understand the market for you to sell to in order to hit your revenue targets.

Second, take note of your competition. Sure, you've managed to pick a market that doesn't already have a strong leader that you have to take on, but that doesn't mean you are alone here. The fact that buyers understand what the market is all about means that there is market demand, and though the market feels uncrowded at the moment, it won't stay that way for long. If you choose to enter this market, you will have to commit to moving quickly to establish yourself as the leader before someone else does. For technology companies, this often means committing to growing your customer base as quickly as you can, which can require outside funding (and the risks and potential headaches that come with that).

If you are looking to bootstrap your business, this may not be the way you want to enter the market.
But if you have clear differentiators and are planning on raising money, this can be a path to winning a very big market.

The work of Head to Head
If you are already the market leader, you need to continually reinforce to your buyers that the current way of thinking about

the market is the best one. This work includes reinforcing the current buying criteria and reiterating why you are the best to deliver those things. You need to quickly and forcefully defend against competitors who attempt to convince buyers to pay attention to other, emerging criteria. You also need to continually demonstrate why you deliver on these criteria better than anyone else in the market.

If you are fighting to unseat a leader in an existing category using the currently established criteria, you're in a battle to prove that you can beat the leader at their own game. You have to clearly demonstrate to the market that you have a superior ability to deliver, and you need to support that claim with hard evidence and undeniable facts.

The good news: if you position yourself in an existing market, you don't have to teach buyers too much about the category itself and you can rely on what they already know.

The bad news: if you rely on what buyers already know, you need to fit within their existing definition if you want to win. software can identify people for security reasons or count people coming in and out of a venue; many would-be buyers of this software know about these solutions. There's an assumption that you could count people fast enough to handle a normal flow of traffic into a retail store or an office building. If your software doesn't do that but is amazing at other things (e.g., at identifying a person against a watch list), then your offering might be a good solution for a subset of the market (the Bigger Fish, Smaller Pond style that we will talk about next) but not a potential winner across the entire market for facial-recognition solutions.

If you choose to use the Head to Head style...

Be prepared to battle against multiple competitors who will be simultaneously trying to prove they are better than you are at the currently established buying criteria, as well as others who are trying to redefine the purchase criteria to their advantage.

> **Positioning Story: My startup transforms our crummy database into a kickass data warehouse**
>
> In Part I, I outlined how my company repositioned its main offering from a "database" to a "data warehouse." Let's examine that positioning shift through the lens of the Head to Head style.
>
> When the company was formed, we thought of our product as a database, so we positioned it as a database. The market category of database, however, was very well established with a clear market leader (Oracle) and a clear set of expected features and pricing. Unknowingly, by calling ourselves a "database" we were announcing to the world that we had the intention of beating Oracle in the overall database market. It shouldn't have been a surprise that the first question we got from every prospect was, So how are you better than Oracle? The expectation was that we sold a database just like Oracle's database, so if we were getting into this business we should have everything their database had, only better. We obviously didn't have that! While we believed we were better at Oracle for certain uses for certain buyers, we clearly weren't a better

general-purpose database than Oracle. As a startup, we could not credibly compete in this market, let alone win it.

Later, we focused on our real competitive differentiator, which was our patented way of doing analysis on a large amount of data. Thinking about our ability to do analytics led us to reposition ourselves as a data warehouse—a completely different market from databases. The data warehousing market at the time was established and most larger companies understood what a warehouse was. Few of them bought warehouses, however; many companies were still developing them in-house because few commercial warehouses existed. For us, this was good news: the demand and market existed but a clear leader did not.

This shift in positioning immediately got us away from trying to compete with Oracle, and it aligned with our strengths. It also had the side benefit of allowing us to raise our prices. Databases at the time were a commodity, but a data warehouse—with fewer options on the market—commanded premium pricing.

2. Big Fish, Small Pond: Positioning to win a subsegment of an existing market

If a market category already exists and there is an existing leader, does that mean you can't compete in that category? Of course not! You may not be able to compete with an established leader head on, but that doesn't mean there isn't a way for you to get a foothold in a piece of the market. Once you do, you can keep expanding your patch until you're established enough to take on a large category leader.

Many startups compete in established market categories and do so successfully by first breaking up the market into smaller pieces and focusing on one piece they can win. In marketing, the process of splitting up an existing market is called subsegmenting. A market can be subsegmented by industry (manufacturing vs. retail), by geographic region (North America vs. South America), company size and a myriad of other criteria.

The goal of the Big Fish, Small Pond style of positioning is to carve off a piece of the market where the rules are a little bit different—just enough to give your product an edge over the category leader.

Like the Head to Head style of positioning, here you are leveraging what buyers already know about the broader market category, but you are calling attention to the fact that some of the requirements for your chosen subsegments are different and not being met by the overall category leader.

You get the advantage of a well-defined category without the stiff competition.

In Head to Head you are attempting to beat Coke in the cola market; in Big Fish, Small Pond, you're selling Coke for dogs. While your product is a lot like Coke (brown and fizzy), it does something that Coke doesn't do and that dogs really, really want (it tastes like bones).

You are not trying to change the purchase criteria for the overall category; in fact, you will have to prove that you do a "good enough" job in those areas when compared with the category leaders. Your focus is showing that there is a subsegment of the overall category with a specific set of needs that the current category leaders are not addressing. Those needs are very important—so important that buyers may want to relax a bit on the overall category criteria to make sure that their subsegment needs are met.

Dominating a small piece of the market is generally much easier than attempting to directly take on a larger leader. From a marketing and sales perspective, smaller subsegments are easier to reach and target, and gaining traction in a market that is more homogeneous is generally easier. List building is easier when you are targeting a subsegment, as is getting in front of groups of prospects. Your value proposition can be highly targeted to these prospects and you will generally have an easier time making your solution's distinct advantages obvious to prospects.

In my experience, one of the best advantages of this style is that once you begin to get traction with some customers, your advantage in the subsegment tends to accelerate quickly. For example, if you are targeting law offices or banks, success with even a single customer is directly applicable to the next customer and can help move the next deal along quickly. Communities also tend to cluster and share information with each other. As you close more business in a particular subsegment, knowledge of your solution in the community will grow quickly because of the links between people in the segment.

Word-of-mouth marketing happens most naturally in tight market subsegments.

A caution here is that the subsegment must represent a large enough opportunity that you can meet your business goals, at least in the short term. Companies tend to shy away from this style because they are worried that moving from targeting the entire market to just a small piece of it will mean less opportunity. In reality the opposite is frequently true: you are simply unselecting the part of the market that was never going to buy your product anyway in order to focus only on customers where you have a distinct advantage. The best way to determine if your chosen subsegment is big enough is to determine how many sales you need to make in the next year to meet your revenue goals. If you need to close thirty deals to make your number this year and your target segment has only one hundred businesses in it, you are going to have to look elsewhere. If, on the other hand, you need to close thirty deals and there are thousands of businesses in your subsegment, it's likely big enough for now.

Just because your initial target market is narrow doesn't mean you will stay narrowly focused forever.

Think back to the lessons in Step 7, about defining a subsegment of best-fit customers for now, and expand that group as the segment and the market evolve. You might start out targeting a very narrow segment but once you have enough customers there, you can start going after adjacent markets where the success you have built so far is relevant. For example, you could start out focusing on credit unions, then expand to retail banks more broadly and then on to other industries like insurance. Once you are larger, you may be ready to take on the market leader head to head, or try to create a new market (more on this in the third style of positioning, Create a New Game).

When to use the Big Fish, Small Pond style

First, this style requires that the category is well defined and there's a clear market leader—and you're not it. People must understand what you mean when you talk about the category. We all know what a vacuum cleaner or a car or bubble gum is, and we understand the basic buying criteria in these categories: vacuum cleaners should have good suction, cars should be reliable, bubble gum should be chewy and capable of blowing great bubbles. If the category is not well understood, subsegmenting it is only going to result in further market confusion.

Second, there needs to be clearly definable groups of customers with unique needs that are not addressed by the market leader. These subsegments may be buyers in a particular industry (banking or legal) or geography (Germany, Latin America), or they may have particular preferences (folks on a gluten-free diet, developers who are certified on Microsoft tools) or ecosystem characteristics (Mac users, marketers who use Eloqua, folks with low internet speed).

The subsegment needs to be easily identifiable—meaning if I had to create a list of prospective buyers, I could figure out a way to do that. For example, I can easily make a list of companies that have more than 1,000 employees by searching the internet for company size info, or a list of Pokémon fans by looking at active users on fan sites or email groups. I would have a much more difficult time creating a list of companies that value design or happy people.

Last, it has to be possible to demonstrate that this sub-segment has a very specific and important unmet need. For example, you might be appealing to companies with workers in very remote places who can't use a solution that requires internet access, or banks in Europe that operate under a different regulatory environment and therefore have different privacy requirements than banks in the United States.

Bic writing itself out of the market

The unmet need must be clearly definable and also important. When Bic launched a "Bic for Her" ballpoint pen that was essentially the same as their other pens, only pink, women reacted first by writing hilarious Amazon reviews (one review starts with, "As a woman, I have been plagued with Man Pen issues for years..."), and then by ignoring the product altogether until it was removed from market for clearly not meeting any specific need of the identified subsegment.

You have the ability to meet the special needs of the subsegment much better than the category leader.

The need of the subsegment must be clearly identifiable, but even when it is, your ability to meet it must be strong enough to convince buyers to go with you over the safer choice of the market leader. These buyers were getting along for the most part by buying a solution that didn't do everything but was likely "good enough" for their business. Convincing them to switch will require showing them that you have deeply understood their specific pain and have fully solved the problem.

The work of Big Fish, Small Pond

This positioning style is often useful for smaller startups that are looking for a way to establish themselves in a market with a strong market leader that they can't take on directly. The work of this style is first to educate the targeted subsegment about how a general-purpose solution is not meeting their needs. You need proof points that show there is a clear gap in value between the general-purpose solution offered by the market leader and your more-purpose-built solution. You need to help the subsegment understand what's in it for them if they do have those needs met. There should ideally be a way to quantify the value to them if they choose your solution over the market leader's more generic solution.

You also have to show that you meet or exceed the existing category criteria (at least the ones that matter most to your subsegment). Remember that you aren't redefining the category, you are merely trying to capture a piece of it, so while you are leading with your defining features and value for your subsegment, you still have to prove that you meet the underlying basic needs common to the overall market category.

If you choose to use the Big Fish, Small Pond style . . .

Understand that the subsegment must have truly distinct needs not being met by the leader in the broader market. If you are trying to dominate a subsegment, be careful that the market leader doesn't turn their attention to the subsegment and try to offer a "good enough" solution with some features that at least partially meet the buyers' needs. Large category leaders will often acquire small companies to block a fast-growing competitor from gaining on them in a particular subsegment. Ideally your competitive advantage is something that is difficult for the market leader to copy, either because you own the intellectual property, or (more commonly) because trying to match your functionality might cause them damage in the broader market where they are winning. It would be difficult for Coke to make a product aimed at dogs without suffering some damage to the perception of the brand among humans.

Positioning Story: A niche CRM startup outpowers a global market leader

I worked at a startup called Janna Systems in the CRM market. In its early days, the company had attempted to sell a contact manager directly to consumers, but improvements to free contact managers from Microsoft, Apple and others quickly destroyed this market. The company moved to selling a CRM solution to businesses and eventually settled on large enterprises as their target market—a very big market.

A couple years after entering the CRM market, Janna Systems was struggling to grow. The enterprise CRM market at that time was completely dominated by one large company, Siebel Systems, which had over $2 billion annual revenue and hundreds of large enterprise customers. (Salesforce, which leads this market today, was a small company back then and focused only on small businesses, not large enterprises—choosing to stick to a submarket rather than have a head-to-head battle against Siebel in the broader category.) Given Siebel's complete dominance in the market, every time we pitched our solution to a company, the first question we had to answer was, How are you better than Siebel? It was a question we struggled to answer.

For the vast majority of our prospects, our differentiators couldn't make up for what Siebel had and we didn't have: a proven solution used by a long list of Fortune 1000 clients; a product with thousands of features that appealed to customers in a wide range of industries; and a famously successful CEO who wrote books, keynoted conferences and appeared regularly on television. In contrast, our product was largely unproven, our feature list was much shorter and our scrappy little team in Toronto was utterly unknown. We charged less than Siebel did, of course, but most large companies cared more about having a product that met their needs than getting a bargain. Once a senior technical manager at a large telco, after listening to our pitch, summed up our positioning as a "cheaper, crappier Siebel." Ouch.

We did, however, have one feature that Siebel didn't. Our CRM let us model relationships between people in a way that Siebel (or any other CRM on the market) couldn't. We always highlighted this feature and included a demonstration in our product demos. The problem was that, in general, customers didn't seem to care about it.

We had a differentiator, but we struggled to map that differentiator to real value for a defined set of prospects.
That changed when we managed to get a sales meeting with the head of investment banking at a very large New

York investment bank. Unlike many of our other prospects, he got really excited when we showed him our special feature. We quickly closed a deal with the bank. In working with them, we began to understand that our little feature solved a serious problem for investment bankers charged with driving business. By using our solution, they were able to unlock significant revenue. We wondered if other investment banks operated the same way. It turned out they did, and the more we spoke to investment banks, the more we understood our product was valuable to them in a way it wasn't for businesses that weren't as deeply driven by relationships.

We began to have a conversation internally about repositioning ourselves away from "enterprise CRM" to positioning ourselves as "CRM for investment banks." At first this shift in positioning seemed risky. Some people on the team felt that moving from focusing on a very large market to a very small one would stifle our growth. Our investors worried that the target market was simply too small for us and we would never grow to be the large company they needed us to be.

At the same time, there was good reason to reposition ourselves. Investment banks continued to call Siebel before they called us, because we still appeared to be delivering more or less the same thing for the same very broad market. Our investment banking clients didn't want their competitors knowing they used our solution, so as not to give them the upper hand, and they refused to let us reference them by name in our marketing materials. Labeling ourselves as

CRM for investment banking gave us a way to put all the attention on our key differentiating feature and signal that we were, in fact, completely different from Siebel. Besides, it wasn't like we were flooded with prospects anyway. We reasoned that even if we positioned ourselves for banks in the short term, we could always expand it to include similar industries (insurance, retail banking) once we had done as much business as we could do with the banks. We decided to give CRM for investment banks a try.

The result was transformational.

Our sales and marketing teams, focused only on investment banks and began to deeply understand the nuances of the that segment's needs. We used banking terms in our pitches, and our demo data looked like banking data. We were still compared with Siebel, but we began to quickly eliminate them as a competitor as we demonstrated that even though they were the best CRM for enterprises, they weren't the best CRM for investment banks.

We raised our prices and began to rapidly close very large deals with investment banks, first in the US and then globally in the UK, Switzerland and Australia, growing our revenue from $2 million to over $70 million in eighteen months.

As we started to expand beyond banking, Siebel began to see us as a legitimate competitive threat and we were acquired for a staggering $1.7 billion, making us the largest acquisition of a Canadian software company at the time.

Not bad for a "cheaper, crappier Siebel" and proof that focusing on a niche doesn't mean you can't grow.

3. Create a New Game:
Positioning to win a market you create

Sometimes new technology or circumstances pave the way for a completely new market. Other times a market can be created by combining one or more existing markets to form one with different buying criteria. Developing a new market comes with its own distinct set of opportunities and challenges.

When to use the Create a New Game style
Because this style of positioning is so difficult, it should only be used when you have evaluated every possible existing market category and concluded that you cannot position your offering there, because doing so would fail to put the focus on your true differentiators and value. This style can also work if your company is large and powerful enough to capture the attention of customers, media and analysts to make a case for why the new market category deserves to exist.

You aren't simply capturing demand that already exists; you have to spark some demand first.
This style is usually only possible when there has been a massive change with a big potential impact on what is possible or what is important in a market. These changes can include new technologies, economic changes, political forces or a combination of these. We saw new markets emerge as cellular networks increased their speeds and coverage, making it possible to do things on a smartphone we couldn't before. Government regulations in privacy and security, particularly in banking and insurance, have driven a wave of data security

and customer-tracking software innovation over the past two decades. Our shifting attitudes about privacy and community facilitated the rise of open social networks like Facebook and Twitter, and the backlash against the unintended consequences of heavy use of those platforms has, in turn, begun to transform our attitudes and preferences around privacy and security.

Often a category emerges when an enabling technology, a shift in customer preferences and a supporting ecosystem manage to come together at once.
If your product cannot be well positioned in any existing category, this might be a good option for you. If your solution requires both a new way of thinking about the boundaries of an existing category *and* a new way of thinking about purchase criteria, then it probably makes more sense to create an entirely new category rather than attempt to stretch existing categories along more than one dimension.

The work of Create a New Game

Creating a new category is the most difficult style of positioning, even when the pre-existing conditions are aligned to support it, mainly because it involves the greatest amount of "teaching" the customer. In the other positioning styles, you're leveraging what folks already know about a category and building on that to create a position in the mind of customers. In this style, you are starting with a blank canvas.

Customers need to first understand why the category deserves to exist. Why is the problem unique? Why do existing solutions in other categories fall short of solving that problem? While you are convincing the market that this category should exist, you are also teaching folks how to best evaluate solutions in that category. And while you are busy with all of that, you need to teach people why you are unquestionably the best vendor to deliver solutions in this category.

To credibly create a new category, you need a product that is demonstrably, inarguably new and different from what exists in other market categories.
Wishful thinking won't convince prospects that you don't belong in any other existing category—this needs to be obviously true in the minds of customers. Also, be aware that the leaders of existing categories may claim that your new product is merely a feature or subset of their existing solutions. To successfully create a new category, you need to have strong arguments against any competitor that tries to convince customers that what you are selling is "merely a feature" instead of a product in its own right.

Timing is also important in creating a new category. To help customers make sense of why this category hasn't emerged sooner, there should be a very strong answer to the questions, Why now? What factors have finally made this category possible and/or necessary? These might be new technology capabilities, a shift in buyer behavior, a change in the business environment such as new government regulations or a shift in the economy.

Category creation is about selling the market on the problem first, rather than on your solution.
If the category doesn't already exist, it means customers aren't currently aware that they have a problem. They don't understand the cost of not solving that problem, nor do they understand the potential value they can unlock by solving that

problem. Customers need to be aware of those things before you can successfully convince them to purchase any solution (including yours).

This style is very, very difficult to execute, but if you manage to pull it off, the rewards are massive.
Unlike the other positioning styles, Create a New Game allows you to create a market that is perfectly tailored to your strengths and weaknesses. It allows you to set the boundaries of the market exactly where you want them and to define purchase criteria so they map exactly to the things you do best. Anyone who successfully defines a market can become its leader because the market was specifically designed that way. Once the market is created, it takes serious work to change it in the minds of customers. Companies that successfully create a category in the customers' minds are well set up to lead it, not only in the short term but also in the future.

This style is the most difficult because it involves dramatically shifting the way customers think, and shifting customer thinking takes a very strong, consistent, long-term effort. That means you need a certain amount of money and time to convince the market to make this shift. Because of the investment and time required, this style is generally best used by more established companies with massive resources to put toward educating the market and establishing a leadership position. For smaller companies, this style generally requires the participation of deep-pocketed, patient investors.

If you choose to use the Create a New Game style...
Follow a long-term plan. At every step, you need to defend yourself as the category leader, or risk having a competitor with

more resources and name-brand recognition reap the rewards of your hard work in creating the category. The most common way startups fail at this style is by working to build the market and then losing out on establishing themselves as its leader. At the exact moment when prospects start to show signs of understanding the category, a larger competitor or a well-funded fast follower swoops in to take advantage of their category-creation work and steal leadership from them.

Positioning Story: Eloqua creates a market category

In the late 1990s Mark Organ was a consultant at Bain & Company researching what made some sales reps perform better than others. His research showed that what made a salesperson really successful was more than just the hiring process or training—the best reps were successful because the company had figured out a way to give them really good leads.

This insight spawned the birth of a startup, Eloqua, in 2000. "The original idea was that we would give reps a way to chat with prospects as they clicked around a company's website. This was not popular with quota-carrying sales professionals, but when we added email marketing functionality, the reps could then track prospects who clicked through and browsed the website. Marketers could send email to prospects, and sales reps could follow up on the leads who exhibited buying behavior online. This MVP (minimally viable product) took off. The people who were most attracted to our ideas referred to themselves not as

"The future isn't a place we are going to go, it's a place we get to create."

NANCY DUARTE

• • • • • • • • • • • • • •

marketers, but 'demand generators.'" These folks were different from the brand marketers who were more commonly found at the time. They were obsessed with funnel metrics and repeatable process, and they focused on generating a stream of qualified leads for the sales team. Mark recognized that what he was providing was an automated way to do that. "We became very focused on serving just these 'demand gen' folks very well and we built the product out for them very specifically. We called it 'demand generation automation' which worked great with our target buyers. Unfortunately, investors and industry analysts couldn't understand what we were. We didn't fit neatly into an existing marketing category the way they had defined it. They thought we were unfocused, by providing a little website tracking, a little email, a little business process automation," says Mark. "They also all thought our market was way too small to be an attractive area to invest or provide industry coverage."

Then the market started to shift. Around 2005, as marketing and sales teams got more mature in their processes, the number of people focused on demand generation started to explode, and so did Eloqua's revenue. "We had created a new category of software in what looked like a tiny market. Suddenly our market was growing very fast and we grew along with it." Investors started to get it and Eloqua finally raised a round of financing, after fourteen quarters of profitability. The company began to grow faster on a larger base of revenue.

Through 2006, the market continued to mature and as demand generation folks proliferated, so did the number of platforms offering email automation and, unfortunately, email spam. "We recognized that customers who bought us for our process automation features were our best customers. They used us as a strategic marketing platform as opposed to a tactical email campaign engine. The deal sizes were significantly bigger; these more strategic customers rarely churned. We shifted our positioning from 'demand generation automation' to the broader term 'marketing automation' to help make our value more obvious and to differentiate ourselves more clearly from simple email automation."

Eloqua grew from around $12 million revenue in 2006 when they first introduced "marketing automation" to $96 million in 2012 when they went public and were shortly after acquired by Oracle for $870 million. Mark says, "The most successful efforts in category creation do not result from company executives creating an acronym at an offsite. Rather they are discovered from deeply understanding a narrow set of customers. These customers are often 'freaks,' extreme in their attitudes and behavior, forged by tectonic technological and societal shifts. The category then emerges when and if the freakish attitudes and behavior become mainstream. Category creation is hard, slow work, but if you are successful the rewards are huge."

STEP 9.
Layer On a Trend (but Be Careful)

Once you have determined your market context, you can start to think about how you can layer a trend on top of your positioning to help potential customers understand why your offering is important to them right now. This step is optional but potentially really powerful— if you go about it carefully.

Think of your product's strengths, your market context and a trend that is relevant to your customer base as three overlapping circles. You are aiming for the center, where all three intersect.

At one point, I worked at a startup that sold a product for retail sales associates that gave them access to information across both e-commerce and in-store systems. The product was positioned in the market as a solution that helped retail sales associates serve customers better. When we talked to retailers, one trend that everyone was interested in was "mobility"—every retailer believed they would need tablets for sales associates in every store in the near future, but they weren't exactly sure how they were going to support that. We used this mobility trend as a jumping-off point to talk about our solution for sales associates, because access to information across multiple platforms and devices—including tablets—was an obvious way that retailers could use mobility to empower their sales associates.

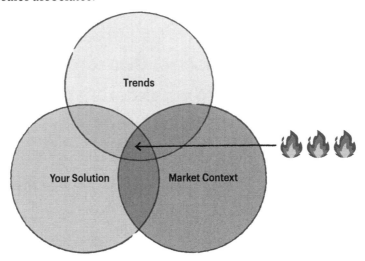

A product that is well positioned in a market can still be very successful without relating it to a trend. Ideally, if a current trend helps reinforce your positioning and the value that your offerings deliver, you can use it to your advantage. Aligning with a trend can help make your offering look current and relevant, particularly for customers interested in that trend. I've worked on many products that were considered useful and valuable and sold quite well, even though they were fundamentally "boring." The use of a relevant trend is not a prerequisite for success, but trends can sometimes give "boring" products an extra gloss of interest. Caution: if the trend doesn't reinforce your positioning, it can also muddy your positioning waters.

It's always better to be a little boring than completely baffling.

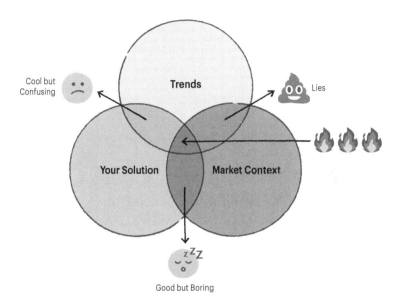

Positioning Story: Redgate Software makes a boring but profitable market cool—and even more profitable

Redgate Software is based in Cambridge, UK. They've been in business since 1999 and are the leader in the database tools market—providing services including data monitoring, synchronization, data privacy and automation. They have over 800,000 users, which means your company is likely a Redgate customer.

Redgate has dozens of products in the market and they wanted to do a better job of telling a story of how customers could see more value by using the products together. Although business was great, customers didn't always see Redgate's products as an urgent or strategic (or dare we say it, *cool*) purchase.

For Redgate, a shift in market category didn't really make sense—their category was well established and they were a leader in it. But that doesn't mean they couldn't spice it up a little by aligning what they do with industry trends.

Redgate noticed that DevOps concepts (software development, or Dev, plus IT operations, or Ops) were gaining in popularity with the development teams they worked with, but it seemed that nobody was talking about the important role of databases in a DevOps transformation—particularly at a time when new data privacy regulations had customers concerned about data security and compliance. So they wove "database DevOps" into their positioning by creating content that described the importance of data in a DevOps transformation and by training their sales team on how to consult with more senior-level folks in a development team that were looking for ways to be smarter about implementing DevOps processes.

The result was a dramatic increase in customers buying multiple Redgate products at a time and a whopping 100% increase in inbound leads (companies contacting Redgate wanting to buy their products)—a clear indicator that Redgate's products had become a higher-priority purchase.

"If you change the way you look at things, the things you look at change."

WAYNE DYER

. . . .

Describing a trend without declaring a market can make your product cool but baffling.

There are lots of ways that throwing trends into the mix can be potentially harmful. Companies can get too focused on the trend to the exclusion of the market, which ultimately leads to confused customers. It's like describing why you are interesting without first telling people who you are. One example was a company that described its app to me as, "the sharing economy for pets." I thought about my own dog and couldn't imagine sharing him with anyone. When I told them I really didn't understand what that was, they switched to describing themselves as "Uber for cats." For a moment I thought about the possibility that these Silicon Valley engineers had succeeded in teaching cats how to drive. "Would they hit the brakes if a dog ran across the street?" I wondered. As enticing as Uber for cats was to me, it seemed unlikely that this was really what the product was all about either. After a bit of probing, they explained that their solution was a marketplace for pet services, like pet sitters and groomers, where customers could find, purchase and rate pet service providers. Once I understood what market they were in, it was much easier to understand what they did. In this case, "sharing economy" is not a market, it's a trend. Uber is also not a market, it's a company (and one that not everyone has consistent assumptions about).

Trends can only be used when they have a clear link to your product. Start by making the connection between your product and the market obvious.

Another way that using trends can get you in trouble is if you focus on the trends and the market, but don't show the link to your actual solution. One example of this is companies that get a little carried away with blogging and other forms of content creation—they are so busy writing content to attract readers that they forget there is an actual solution their company sells. While the trend might be fun to read about, it doesn't help to sell any product.

When the company Long Island Iced Tea made the radical decision to change its name to Long Blockchain (really), it made headlines for days while investors and analysts tried to draw a link between their iced tea and this hot, new technology trend. The stock briefly soared as the company made little effort to explain how exactly it would exploit blockchain for its business, but that didn't deter blockchain enthusiasts from speculating about all of the potential ways that an injection of blockchain magic might transform even a boring business that sold iced tea. Over the course of a couple weeks, however, it become clear that Long Blockchain didn't have a blockchain strategy to go with the name change—no new partnerships, no explanation of how blockchain would be used and no clear relationship between their existing business and any potential new business related to blockchain. Once investors realized this disconnect, the stock plummeted and within months the company was delisted from the Nasdaq stock exchange, proving that trying to capitalize on hype without linking it to your product is a dangerous game.

If you find that you don't have a way to pull trends into your positioning, there's no need to panic. Many companies operate perfectly fine in markets that don't have much sizzle and pizzazz. There's something to be said for tried and true, even traditional. If there's a way to pull in trends, you should do it, but if there isn't, it's possible to have a very successful business without being trendy in the slightest.

STEP 10.
Capture Your Positioning so It Can Be Shared

Positioning on its own isn't useful to a company. Once you have worked through your positioning, you need to share it across the organization. Positioning needs to have company buy-in so it can be used to inform branding, marketing campaigns, sales strategy, product decisions and customer-success strategy.

One of my biggest complaints about the positioning statement was that the statement itself was too brief to communicate the subtleties of a product's position, and at the same time was too contrived and awkward to be memorized or repeated. I recommend capturing your positioning in a document with enough detail that it can be used by marketing, sales and product creation. This document should break down each individual component of the position, give enough detail for each to be understood and show how they interact with one another.

I'm a fan of having a shorter, concise version of the positioning that can be captured on a single page and easily shared across the company. I also try to capture the positioning at a higher level in a positioning canvas.

Here's the positioning canvas I use. It includes the product name and a one-line description as well as the market category (and subcategory if needed). It then lets you line up competitive alternatives, attributes, value and customer segments in a way that shows the relationship between them.

Table 2. Positioning canvas

Product name and one-line description			
Market category (and subcategory) The macro market and submarket (if applicable) that you compete in			
Competitive alternatives What would customers use if your product did not exist?	**Unique attributes** What features/ capabilities does your product have that the alternatives do not?	**Value** What value do those attributes enable for customers?	**Who cares a lot** What are the characteristics of a customer that makes them care a lot about the value you deliver?

I have a template for a positioning document and a version of the positioning canvas that you can download at aprildunford.com.

III

PUTTING POSITIONING INTO PLAY

AFTER POSITIONING: WHAT HAPPENS NEXT?

When I run positioning workshops with startups, as soon as we have completed the 10-step process, I usually get the question, "OK, April, now what?"

A positioning exercise on its own is valuable, in particular when it gets the entire team to agree on what the differentiated value is for the offering and what customer segments the sales and marketing teams should be targeting. The next stage is to make the positioning real across the company. How do you implement a position? The most obvious immediate next thing after a change in positioning is to create new messaging that reflects the positioning. Interestingly, however, having worked with dozens of companies on their positioning, I've found that before we tackle messaging, it is more effective to craft what I call a "sales story."

Translating Your Positioning into a Sales Story

Most of the companies I work with sell to businesses, and even more specifically, they have a complex sales cycle that involves a salesperson talking to a prospect at least once before they can close a sale. For these types of businesses, it's very important that the positioning is embodied in the way your salespeople frame the product, particularly on a first sales call. As a group, once you have completed a positioning exercise, you can work through defining a story of how a salesperson would pitch the product. This doesn't mean you will be creating the exact copy that will go in the presentation, nor will you be working on making that presentation look good. You can think of this as more of an exercise where you define the components of a sales story that will later be worked into an actual presentation for the sales team to use.

When selling to businesses, a sales story generally follows a common arc. It starts with a definition of the problem that your solution was designed to solve. As a team you can succinctly define the problem your solution solves. In a final sales presentation, the definition of the problem helps to put a boundary around the discussion and frame it in a way that makes what you are talking about obvious to customers as well. An example would be, "Insurance companies today are trying to make their claims process less difficult for demanding digital-savvy customers," or "Cash flow is critical to small businesses where an unexpected expense can kill a company."

The story then moves to describing how customers are attempting to solve the problem today and where the current solutions fall short. Using the previous examples this might be, "Insurers have added mobile claims functionality, but it still requires customers to do many steps of the process manually," or "Some small businesses can get financing from their bank, but many do not qualify, and getting a bank loan takes time."

The next stage of the story is what I call "the perfect world." It's where you describe what the features of a perfect solution would be, knowing what you know about the problem and the limitations of current solutions. In our examples it would be something like, "In a perfect world, customers could complete the entire claims process seamlessly with their mobile device," or "In a perfect world, small businesses could get the money they need quickly based on business they have already closed."

The sales story goes on to introduce the product or company and position it in the relevant market category. For example, "Mobileclaimsorama is a mobile claims management solution for insurers," or "Financialhoohah offers invoice financing to growing small businesses."

Next, the story naturally flows into talking about each of the value themes with a bit more detail into how the solution enables that value. A completed sales deck also adds some information, such as handling common objections, a case study or list of current customers. The story wraps up with a discussion of whatever you would like the prospect to do next.

The point of working through the sales story is that everyone in the discussion can agree on how the positioning translates into a "pitch." To do that, the team needs to agree on how to define the problem, current solutions, the gap and the key purchase criteria that a customer should have when looking for a solution in your market.

I have an outline and a template for a typical sales story that you can download at aprildunford.com.

Messaging

While the sales story can be mapped out with a team, messaging is not something you want to do in real time with a group.

Once the story arc is complete, the marketing team will translate that into messaging that can be used in marketing and sales materials, for campaigns and on the website.

There are already stores full of books that can teach you how to do a better job of messaging, so I will give you just one tip that I think is important: write a messaging document. Every campaign you create or new piece of material you build is going to have a slightly different purpose and slightly different messaging. If there isn't one master messaging document that is used as the starting point, your messaging (and often your positioning) will start to creep as messages are built on modified messages in a chain. A messaging document helps you keep a record of the accepted baseline messaging, gives everyone a common starting point for building specific copy for a specific purpose and keeps the language (and the positioning) from evolving too far away from the agreed-upon starting point.

I have a messaging document template that I give my clients and you can download at aprildunford.com.

Product Roadmap and Pricing

A change in positioning usually impacts marketing and sales first but it often has impacts well beyond that. Changing the way the company thinks about itself will usually have an impact on how product features get prioritized in the future. It makes sense that the roadmap for "accounting software" would look really different from the roadmap for "financial services." Great positioning is usually strengthened over time with adjustments in features.

Similarly, pricing reflects positioning and might need to be adjusted. There are price expectations in each market category, so getting your pricing in line with those will help reinforce that your product belongs there. For example, we raised the pricing for our "CRM for investment banks" because our investment banking customers didn't expect us to be the same price as a general-purpose CRM.

While most people think of positioning as a marketing concept, a shift in positioning feels more like a shift in business strategy. Every department inside the company is likely to be impacted over time.

Tracking Your Positioning over Time

Both products and markets change over time. Companies need to regularly check in on their positioning and adjust it as technology and landscapes evolve. I recommend checking in on your positioning every six months or when there has been a major event that could impact the competitive landscape or the way customers perceive and evaluate solutions.

A sudden change in the competitive landscape could signal a need to adjust your positioning.
There are a host of ways that a change in the competitive landscape can weaken your position. The most common change happens when a credible, established competitor enters your market. Large competitors have the ability to reach a very large number of prospects in a short amount of time, through marketing spend, sales channels and partnerships. Credible competitors can quickly change prospects' perceptions about what is possible for offerings in the space, which features matter most, what the expected pricing should be and more. Some competitors have the ability to purchase an up-and-coming company in the space and give it the additional

support capacity, partnerships and sales reach it previously lacked, making a once-small player suddenly very credible as a contender to lead a market.

The addition of a large, potentially threatening competitor doesn't necessarily mean your positioning should change. For example, if your strategy was to target a subsegment of the market, it's possible a larger competitor isn't going to serve that segment any better than the current market leader. What matters most in these situations is customers' perceptions. Do your target customers expect this new competitor to be relevant to them? Do they expect a change in the market (e.g., a price drop or a change in expected features) now that this competitor has arrived? If they don't, then your position shouldn't need to change.

If the arrival of a competitor does signal a change in the way customers think about a market, then you will have to revisit your positioning. Start at Step 4, considering your competitive alternatives. Has that list shifted in the minds of your best customers? If so, does that change your key unique attributes and the value you can deliver?

Other outside forces can also change your market.
New competitors aren't the only factor that can upset your positioning. Outside forces can swing markets in ways that are often difficult to predict.

Government regulations can suddenly force customers to care about features that previously weren't important at all and can give one competitor an edge over another. Sometimes even the threat of an impending regulatory change can be enough to shift a market. In the two decades I've worked in tech, I've seen security and privacy regulations sweep through banking and insurance, and later through manufacturing and retail, in a

"If you want success, be unique."

NATALIE MASSENET

• • • • • • • • • • • • • • • •

way that few of us predicted. Each time, there were companies that managed to strengthen their positions as those changes took place, and other companies that couldn't cope with the changes and fell by the wayside.

Big changes in the economic climate can impact your positioning in obvious and less-than-obvious ways. During economic downturns, business customers generally shift their focus from pushing hard to expand revenue to cost cutting and cash conservation. Vendors selling into business with a strong position related to growing revenue often find themselves having to adjust that positioning toward costs savings (or vice versa) as their customers' priorities change.

New technology can suddenly change what is possible in a market. Once customers understand it, purchase criteria can shift very quickly.

For example, here in North America, the move from 3G to 4G and LTE cell networks suddenly allowed consumers to stream video and movies on a mobile device. Users shifting to LTE devices in North America relied less on Wi-Fi connectivity, and mobile data usage skyrocketed. Now suppose you sell a marketing automation solution and you already support video marketing. That feature, which may have been less important in the past, could become a critical point of differentiation between you and your competitors, should you choose to emphasize it in your positioning.

The attitudes and preferences of customers can shift over time.

Variable customer attitudes can be the hardest factor to track in your market, but you can generally spot the warning signs and see the potential causes of a shift in buying pattern if you know how to look for them. We don't generally think of business buyers as being highly susceptible to shifts in personal preferences, but I have proof that they can be. I worked at a startup that sold a software pre-installed on a server to technical buyers that would have these servers in their data centers. We were a deeply technical team and our offering was a patented solution for deeply technical buyers. We never worried about what those servers *looked* like—nobody cared! Or so we thought.

On a business trip to New York, I was invited to tour a large bank's data center, and the CIO walked right past millions of dollars of racks of non-descript server hardware from IBM to point out a little appliance that he had just purchased from a scrappy startup. "Look at the cool purple lights!" he exclaimed. "I never get to show anyone anything that actually looks cool, but I love this thing!" Within a year, everyone selling bundled hardware and software were packaging their product in jazzy-looking server boxes and talking about "design" in a way they had never done previously in the data center business.

CONCLUSION

For the first few years of my career, it felt like positioning products was akin to influencing fate. A hidden power appeared to control the destiny of those products—one part buyer impulses, one part market chaos and one part dumb luck.

Gradually, I learned that I could influence positioning a little, and as I got smarter at it, I could influence it a lot. The more I talked with other executives working on launching new products into a market, the more I could see the patterns of what worked and what didn't, and my own skill at positioning improved. Yours can too.

You've read this book, which puts you much further ahead of where I was about midway through my career as a marketing executive. You have a clear, 10-step process for positioning any product, including three positioning styles you can use depending on your market. I want to leave you with some key takeaways:

1. **Any product can be positioned in multiple markets.** Your product is not doomed to languish in a market where nobody understands how awesome it is.

2. **Great positioning rarely comes by default.** If you want to succeed, you have to determine the best way to position your product. Deliberate, try, fail, test and try again.

3. **Understanding what your best customers see as true alternatives to your solution will lead you to your differentiators.**

4. **Position yourself in a market that makes your strengths obvious to the folks you want to sell to.**

5. **Use trends to make your product more interesting to customers right now, but be very cautious.** Don't layer on a trend just for the sake of being trendy—it's better to be successful and boring, rather than fashionable and bewildering.

Knowing how to do something is not the same as understanding how to teach someone else how to do it. As leaders, we often become very good at *doing* things that we have a very hard time explaining to the teams that work with us. This book is my attempt to codify and teach one of the most complicated processes I've learned to do in my career. I sincerely hope it offers you a shortcut to better position your products to succeed.

ABOUT THE AUTHOR

April Dunford is an executive consultant, speaker and author who helps technology companies make complicated products easy for customers to understand and love. She is a globally recognized expert in positioning and market strategy, and has launched sixteen products into market across her twenty-five-year career as VP of marketing at a series of successful, high-growth startups. April advises leadership, sales and marketing teams through training, workshops and keynote talks. She is also a board member, investor and advisor to dozens of high-growth businesses.

www.aprildunford.com

Work with April Dunford to Take Your Customers from "What?" to "WOW!"

The sad truth is that we will not buy what we do not understand. And prospects are drowning in a sea of innovations, with each new product claiming to be uniquely valuable. How can we help prospects grasp something they have never seen before?

Positioning is a secret superpower that, when harnessed correctly, can change the way the world thinks about a problem, a technology or even an entire market. And April Dunford is your company's secret weapon. As a globally recognized positioning consultant, April has worked with executive teams at both startups and global technology companies to ensure that customers can intuitively understand the magic of their innovations.

Learn how to make your product obviously awesome

Through one- or two-day sessions or customized workshops, April will teach you and your team a practical methodology that will make your product value shine.

The two-day positioning workshop for startups

Using the methodology outlined in this book and field-tested with dozens of startups, April offers a facilitated intensive workshop that will nail the best positioning for your product or company. The workshop will give your team a framework for understanding how customers make sense of products and will guide you through a blueprint for positioning your product or company so that the value is obvious to your best-fit prospects. April also helps you take that positioning and break it down into a "sales story" that your sales team can immediately begin to use with customers. Fast-paced and challenging, this workshop is an accelerated way to get a grip on your positioning and ensure your executive team is all in alignment.

The two-hour course for product and marketing or executive teams

April offers a deep-dive course that is tailored to teams in larger organizations that want to learn more about positioning. Drawing on both her experience as an executive launching sixteen products into market and her experience working with dozens of technology companies both large and small, April delivers an engaging intensive on best practices for positioning. Your team will leave with a methodology, tools and templates that they can immediately apply to both new and in-market products.

The ninety-minute group workshop for startup accelerators and other groups

April frequently delivers group workshops specifically tailored to early-stage startups and founders who do not necessarily come from a marketing or sales background. This session is engaging and fun but also densely packed with information, processes and tools that teams can put to work immediately. Packed with specific examples and startup case studies, this crash course gives founders and their teams a solid foundation of positioning knowledge.

Customized workshops

Has your company made an acquisition that changes the way customers think about your product? Has a new competitor entered your market and shaken things up? Do you have an important new technology that potentially redefines the market? April will design a session from the ground up to work through specific positioning challenges with your team.

"You won't meet anyone that understands the art of positioning as deeply as April. I'm lucky to work with her on the board of a high growth startup. This book is a must-read for anyone looking for a practical positioning primer, like having a virtual April as a sidekick with you at all times—always entertaining and on point."
Michelle McBane, managing director StandUp Ventures and senior investment director MaRS Investment Accelerator Funds

Learn more at www.aprildunford.com

Printed in Great Britain
by Amazon

87631893R00116